PIER PAOLO PASOLINI

POETRY

PIER PAOLO PASOLINI

POETRY

Selected and Translated, with an Afterword, by

ANTONINO MAZZA

TORONTO
Exile Editions
1991

This edition is published by Exile Editions Ltd.,
20 Dale Avenue, Toronto, Ontario, Canada
M4W 1K4

Sales distribution
General Publishing Co. Ltd.
30 Lesmill Road, Don Mills, Ontario M3B 2T6

Designed by LOU LUCIANI
Typeset in STEMPEL GARAMOND
Printed by UNIVERSITY OF TORONTO PRESS

Canadian Cataloguing in Publication Data

Pier Paolo Pasolini, 1922–1975.
Pier Paolo Pasolini: Poetry

Translated from Italian.
Includes bibliographical references.

ISBN 0-920428-73-8

I. Mazza, Antonino. II. Title.
PQ4835.A48P54 1991 851'.914 C92-093063-8

The publisher wishes to acknowledge the assistance towards publication of the Ontario Arts Council

This publication was assisted by the Minister of Foreign Affairs Government of Italy through the Istituto Italiano di Cultura, Toronto, *Director* Francesca Valente

CONTENTS

Part Three

Part Four

Appendix

ACKNOWLEDGEMENT

Acknowledgement is made to the editors and publishers of the following magazines in which some of the translations in this volume originally appeared: The Idler, Anthos, Exile *and* Vice Versa. The First Paradise, Odetta..., *was first published in a limited edition commemorating the tenth anniversary of Pasolini's death, printed on dampened St. Armand handmade paper, using an 8 × 12 Chandler Price Press, by Hugh W. Barclay, Thee Hellbox Press (1985). I am especially grateful to Laura Betti, Associazione Fondo Pier Paolo Pasolini, Graziella Chiarcossi, Nico Naldini and Barry Callaghan for their trust; to Andreas Page, Fraser Sutherland, Gerald Owen, Cy Strom and Prof. Corrado Federici for invaluable editorial suggestions; to Prof. Eli Mandel, Adele Wiseman, Primo Di Luca, Prof. Luigi Lombardo-Satriani, Prof. Vito Teti, Prof. Cesare Pitto, Franca Mazzolani, Francesca Valente, Damiano Pietropaolo, Helen Vukovich and Prof. Franco Loriggio for their amity and encouragement. Treasured is the lasting memory of Prof. Robert F. Harney (1939–1989), of the Multicultural History Society of Ontario, for commending the prophecy. An Ontario Arts Council translation grant aided in the completion of this volume. The publisher and the translator wish to express their appreciation to Aldo Garzanti Editore (c). To my wife, Franceline Quintal, goes all my love for embracing the struggle.*

PIER PAOLO PASOLINI:

TO THE NEW READER[1]

(1970)

The last book of poetry I published, *Poetry in Form of a Rose*, was in 1964. Six years have passed. Since that time I have made several films (from *The Gospel according to Saint Matthew*, which I was working on when *Poetry in Form of a Rose* came out, to *Hawks and Sparrows, Oedipus Rex, Teorema, Porcile* and *Medea*): all these films I have made "as a poet."* It's not the place here to analyze the equivalences that can be found between the "poetic feelings" aroused by certain sequences in my films and similar ones aroused by certain parts of my poetry books. No attempt has ever been made to analyze these equivalences, except in very general terms with reference to content. It can't be denied, however, that a certain *way of feeling something* is repeated *exactly* when reading some of my verses and viewing some of my cinematic shots.

But, from 1964 onward, I have not composed poems through film alone. It was only for a year or two that I was silent as a "verse poet" (even if the poems I wrote have remained largely unpublished or unfinished): in '65 I was sick in bed for a month, and during my convalescence, I began to work again. Perhaps because during my sickness I had reread Plato with a joy that I can't describe, I began to write plays: six verse tragedies, on which I've worked for the past five years – returning to them sometimes after a year or longer – soon to be published with the title *Calderón*.

Evidently, in this period, I could write verses only by attributing them to protagonists who would act as my intermediaries.

* I use this term in its strict "technical" sense.

But, beginning with some occasional verses, some of which were written on commission (after a first poem that had hardly been worked on – "The PCI speaks to the youth!![2] – written in early March of 1968, and published shortly thereafter treacherously without my knowledge, in an illustrated magazine)* in the autumn of that year I again became a "verse maker" in the current sense of the term: and now I have a new volume, *Trans-humanize and Organize*, which will soon be appearing through the same publisher who has now asked me to write this introduction to my "old" poems.

Six years are not many: but if we keep in mind that the first of these volumes here anthologized was published in June '57 (and that the poem "The Ashes of Gramsci"[3] that gave it its title is from May '54), then, the interval of a mere six years becomes the interval of an entire political and poetic era, even if the later poems partly lived through this transition.

I suppose, therefore, that I am addressing a "new reader." To him I can not and do not wish to give anything other than information.

I didn't begin to write verses with *The Ashes of Gramsci*: I began much earlier, precisely in 1929, in Sacile, when I was seven years old, in the second grade.

It was my mother who taught me how a poem can be concretely written, and not just read in school ("Glassy is the air," and all that). Mysteriously, one day my mother presented me with a sonnet, written by herself, in which she expressed her love for me (I can't remember by what rhyme constraints the poem ended with the words "the love I have for you is infinite"). A few days later, I wrote my first verses, where I spoke of a "nightingale" and of "verdure." I don't believe at that time I

* If it had come out in the specialized journal (*Nuovi Argomenti*) for which it was intended, it would have been an altogether different story.

could have distinguished a nightingale from a finch, much less a poplar from an elm tree, nor can I say that at school (in the cares of Signora Ada Costella, a Tuscan, my teacher in that unforgettable second-grade class) we were reading Petrarch.[4] So I don't know where I could have picked up the classical code of linguistic election and selection. The fact remains, however, that, not taking account of my mother's "*abundantia cordis*," I began strictly as a "selective" and "elect" poet.

Since that time, I've written whole collections of verse: at thirteen I was an epic poet (from *The Iliad* to *The Lusiads*). I did not overlook verse drama, and in my adolescence I did not avoid the inevitable encounter with Carducci,[5] Pascoli[6] and D'Annunzio,[7] a phase which began in Scandiano – the high school which I attended as a commuter was in Reggio Emilia – and then was completed in Bologna, at the Liceo Galvani, in 1937, the year in which a substitute teacher, Antonio Rinaldi, read a poem by Rimbaud to the class.

From '37 to '42 or '43, I lived the great period of Hermeticism,[8] studying with Longhi[9] at the university, and living ingenuous literary relations with peers interested in these things, two of whom were Francesco Leonetti[10] and Roberto Roversi;[11] and, though a couple of years older than we, Francesco Arcangeli[12] and then Alfonso Gatto[13] were also part of the group. I was rather precocious to be a university student; but I lived that experience not just as an apprentice but also as an initiate. In 1942, in fact, my first book of poetry, *Poesia a Casarsa* (*Poems of Casarsa*), was published, at my own expense, by the Libreria Antiquaria of Signor Landi: I was exactly twenty, but I had begun to write the poems collected in that slim volume three years earlier in Casarsa,[14] my mother's village, where we went each summer for our vacations with relatives, since my father's meager salary as an officer in the army allowed us only such poor vacations, etc.

They were poems in the Friulian dialect: the *hésitation*

*prolongée entre le sens et le son** had made an apparently definitive choice, favoring sound. The semantic dilation worked upon sound had transferred the semantemes into another linguistic domain, from whence they returned as gloriously indecipherable.

Some fifteen days after the book appeared, I received a postcard from Gianfranco Contini,[15] saying that he liked the book, and would immediately review it.

Who could ever describe my joy? I jumped and danced along the arcades of Bologna. As for the worldly satisfaction that one could aspire to from writing verses, what I felt that day in Bologna was truly complete, so much so that I can forever do without any more of it. Contini's review did not come out then in *Primato*, as he had thought, but in the *Corriere di Lugano*, abroad, in Switzerland, by definition the country of exiles. Why in Switzerland? Because fascism – to my great surprise – did not concede the existence of local particularisms in Italy, thought to be idioms of some obstinate idlers. As such ... my "pure language of poetry" had been mistaken for a realistic document that proved the existence of shoddy eccentric peasants, or at least of peasants ignorant of the idealistic guidelines of the central Authority. ... It is true that I was no longer a "natural" fascist since that day in 1937 when I had heard Rimbaud's poem; but the anti-fascism now ceased to be purely cultural: I was beginning to experience the Evil at first hand.

That winter we took refuge in Casarsa, and 1943 remains for me one of the happiest years of my life: "mi joventud, veinte años en tierra de Castilla!"†

I continued to write poems in Friulian, but I also began to write poems in Italian in a similar style. The Friulian of the poems had now become exactly the language spoken in Casarsa (not the

* Valéry, cited by Jakobson.

† Machado.

Friulian invented with the help of the Pirona dictionary);* while my Italian, being influenced by the dialect, had acquired a Romance-language ingenuous air. Literary Italian – the new Latin, as it was then called, indebted as it was to the Hermeticists, and especially Leopardi – continued nevertheless to impose on me its inescapable elective and selective tradition; so I wrote verses ("Diaries") and kept a journal (a "Notebook" analogous to the "Zibaldone"[16]), which continued to follow a "central thread" begun in privilege long before (and destined never to be severed), even before those Friulian poems that as I said were published in '42: the latter being, therefore, with respect to my earlier ambitious literary production, almost trifles, "*nugae*," in the vulgar language. Except that in the case of these Friulian poems – I don't know by what presumption, but certainly in some way – I felt, though perhaps without daring to admit it even to myself, that it was precisely these "*nugae*" that really mattered.

I was later to publish these Friulian poems with Sansoni, in 1951; while the Italian "*nugae*" that I had begun to write at that time would become *L'Usignolo della chiesa cattolica* (*The Nightingale of the Catholic Church*), published by Longanesi in 1958. Meanwhile, I had been drafted into the army, and was gone a few days, from September 1 to September 8, 1943. I returned from Pisa to Casarsa in rags, one shoe different from the other, after disobeying my officers' orders to surrender arms to the Germans (by a canal near Livorno) – after traveling over one hundred kilometres on foot, risking a thousand times ending up being taken by train to Germany. In Casarsa again I started to write poems in Friulian and in Italian, the rural splendor of *La Meglio Gioventù* (*The Finest Youth*) and *L'Usignolo della chiesa cattolica*. None of this, however, prevented me from writing *Long Live Freedom* on the walls, which landed me for the first

* Friulian-Italian Dictionary.

time in my life in prison, thus experiencing first hand what men of order are all about.

Thereafter, I spent my days in hiding, hunted – terrorized, because at that time I was haunted by a decidedly pathological fear of death – obsessed by the idea that I would end up hanged on a hook: this was in fact what happened to youths on the Adriatic coast who resisted the draft or declared themselves anti-fascists. My brother – three years my junior, and now of draft age – left for the mountains to be an armed partisan: I accompanied him to the train station (a gun hidden in a book). He was leaving as a communist; later, taking my advice (my having lived three years more than he under fascism must have counted for something in his eyes) he jointed the Osoppo Division of the Action Party:[17] some communists tied to Tito, who wanted to annex part of Friuli, would later kill him.

The war ended, and so began the most tragic period of my life (I went on writing *La Meglio Gioventù* and *L'Usignolo*): my brother's death and my mother's superhuman grief; my father's homecoming from his wartime prison, a sick veteran, poisoned by the defeat of fascism in his country and the defeat of the Italian language in his home – a ferocious wreck, a tyrant with no remaining power, crazed even more by too much bad wine, more than ever in love with my mother who had never truly reciprocated in her love for him, and who now moreover was intent only on her grief; and on top of this, add the problem of my life and of my flesh. In the winter of '49, my dear reader (particularly dear to me because you are new, and because you go for these simple anthologies in inexpensive editions) I escaped with my mother to Rome, as in a novel.

The Friulian period had ended; the poems would long remain in the drawer, till the time they were published, as I stated above; but once in Rome I immediately began again to write those diaries, in a verse that was far less eccentric, in a literary post-Hermetic vein, that, as I have said, I had never stopped writing, even in that Romance-Friulian language among the vineyards and mulberry trees. I collected a first sample of them under the title *Roma 1950* (and later in *Sonetto Primaverile* (*Springtime Sonnet*), Scheiwiller, 1960). Soon, however, a few months after arriving in Rome, while on the one hand I continued my anti-Italian research in a Baroque and Gaddian key, which I had begun, as I said, in the Romance-Friulian key – I started to write that "thing," a narrative that then would become *Ragazzi di vita* (*The Ragazzi*), published in 1955. In Rome I lived in Piazza Costaguti at first, near the Ottavia Gate (the ghetto!), then I went to live in the suburban ghetto, near the Rebibbia prison, in a house that had been left completely without a roof (thirteen thousand lire per month rent). For two years I was desperately unemployed, not unlike those who end up as suicide statistics; then I found a job teaching in a private school in Ciampino for twenty-seven thousand lire a month. In the house of Rebibbia, a working-class slum, I began a slow transformation and fusion of my anti-Italian research, often in a falsetto voice (that had produced the dialect verses and similar verses in Italian), with the more classicist research of the diaries – what became my truly "poetic oeuvre," that we now call my "old" work, from *The Ashes of Gramsci* to *Poetry in Form of a Rose*.

I have said it so many times, in so many interviews, that it's become almost a mechanism to turn the subject to my own interests (to bend reality to my designs): what pushed me to become a communist was the struggle of the Friulian day-laborers against the landowners that took place immediately after the war ("The Days of Lodo De Gaspari" was to be the title of my first novel, published instead in 1962 with the title *Il sogno di una cosa* (*The Dream of Something*).) I was on the side of the day-laborers. Then, I read Marx and Gramsci.[18]

The transformation and fusion, to which I referred, of my two threads of research, the anti-Italian in falsetto, and the elect Italian, occurs under the influence of my own brand of Marxism which is never orthodox. I arrive at the "civil poem" on Gramsci's ashes very slowly: the entire first part of the book, from "L'Appennino" ("The Apennines") to "L'umile Italia" ("Humble Italy") is prehistoric with respect to it; in the poems of the Roman subproletarian slums, we still find the pre-Alpine spirit of the clean earth, of the cedar forests, that accumulates formally, especially in the obligatory spaces of the necessary rhyme (of the tercets), in the guise of delaying elements. I come to be aware just now that from the time of the struggle of the day-laborers until today, very little has changed within me, and outside of me for that matter. While I write this introduction for a non-specialized reader, I am also working on a documentary on the strike by Roman street cleaners ("Notes for a novel on garbage"), and it doesn't seem to me that things have changed very much in these past thirty years. It could be that the sentiments of the class struggle of the youth of 1968–70 have turned back the clock to those old days: and it matters not if this is an illusion on my part. For the rest, the class struggle is a phenomenon that can't be resolved in thirty years, whose characteristics are always the same.

In conclusion, the poems I selected from the previous volumes comprise the thirteen years from 1951 to 1964 and form a coherent and compact block. What strikes me most about them – this sounds as if I had become alienated from them, which of course isn't at all true – is a diffuse sense of disheartening unhappiness; an unhappiness that is part of the language itself, like a given reducible to a quantity, or even a physicality. This sense (almost a right) of being unhappy, is so predominant, that the same sensual joy (of which after all the book is full, though accompanied by a sense of guilt) is obscured by it; and so is its civil idealism. What strikes me even more, on rereading these poems, is my realization of how ingenuous was the expansiveness with which I wrote them: as if I were writing for someone who could only have a great love for me. I finally understand why I was so distrusted and hated.

PIER PAOLO PASOLINI

POETRY

from THE RELIGION OF MY TIME

Humiliated And Hurt
(1958)

Epigrams

To An Unborn Child

At the other end of that pristine new bridge on the Tiber
completed by the Catholics to satisfy the Fascists,
among the friezes, boundary stones, fake ruins and phoney fragments,
a clutch of women waited for clients in the sun.
Among them there was Franca from Viterbo, only a child, but already a mother:
she ran towards the door of my car, shouting,
she was so sure that I could not disappoint her:
she climbed in, settled comfortably, cheerful as a boy,
and directed me towards the Cassia:[19] we crossed an intersection,
sped along a sun-bathed and deserted road
among limestone craters and wretched stucco houses,
and arrived at her spot: a little field
at the foot of a rise covered with stonecrop and potted with grottoes.
In the distance an old chestnut horse on the damp grass,
an abandoned automobile among the shrubs,
and not very far off, here and there, the festive echo of gunshots:
all around there were couples, young boys, and poor girls.
In those days my life was sure, my work satisfying,
no anxieties, no impending fears about the future:
I had managed for years – at first by means of the physical attributes
of grace, calmness, health and enthusiasm, with which I was born,
later by means of my alert, though uncertain mind – love
strength and conscience, which I acquired through experience.
And yet, my first and only unborn child, I do not grieve
because you can never be here, in this world.

To A Pope

A few days before you died, death
  eyed one of your contemporaries:
at twenty, you were a student, he a laborer,
  you a wealthy nobleman, he a plebeian youngster:
but the same days showered on both of you the radiance
  of ancient Rome emerging anew.
I saw poor Zucchetto's remains.
  One night he was wandering drunk through the Market
    district,
and the San Paolo tram ran him down,
  dragging him along the tracks and through the plane-trees:
for some hours he was left under the wheels:
  a few people gathered to look in silence:
it was late, there was only a handful of passers-by.
  One of those who exist because you exist,
an old policeman dressed like a slovenly thug,
  yelled at anyone who got too close: "Get the hell out of here!"
Then came the ambulance to remove the body:
  the people left, some shreds remained scattered around the site,
and the owner of a nearby all-night café
  a woman who knew the man, said to a late arrival
that Zucchetto had ended up under the wheels of a tram, he was
    gone.
  A few days later you were gone: Zucchetto was one
of your vast, human, Roman flock,
  a poor drunkard, with no family and no place to sleep,
who wandered by night, living who knows how.
  You knew nothing about him: as you knew nothing
about other thousands upon thousands of poor wretches like
    him.

Perhaps it is cruel of me to ask why
people like Zucchetto should be unworthy of your love.
There are repulsive places, where mothers and their babies
live in an ancient dust, in the mud of other epochs.
Not far from where you lived,
in view of Saint Peter's arresting cupola,
there is one such place, the Gelsomino Quarter...
A mountain bisected by a pit, and below,
between a swamp and a row of new buildings,
a heap of pathetic dwellings, not houses but pigsties.
A sign, a gesture, a single word from you would have been enough,
and your children would have had a home:
you didn't bother to make a gesture, say a word.
You were not being asked to forgive Marx! An immense
breaker dividing millennia of life
separated you from him, from his religion:
but in your religion don't they talk of compassion?
During your pontificate thousands of men,
before your very eyes, lived in pens and pigsties.
You knew this. To sin does not mean to do harm:
not to do good, this is what sin is.
How much good might you have done! And didn't bother to:
you the greatest sinner.

New Epigrams
(1958-59)

To Contemporary Men Of Letters

I see you: you exist, we continue to be friendly,
we are happy to recognize and greet one another, in some café,
in the homes of ironic Roman ladies...
But our greetings, the smiles, the usual passions,
are acts taking place in a no man's land: a *waste land*[20]
for you: for me, a margin between one history and another.
We cannot really agree any longer: it makes me shudder.
Within us the world is enemy to the world.

To My Nation

Not an Arabic, not a Balkan, not an ancient people
  but a vital nation, a European nation:
and what are you? Land of starving, corrupted infants,
  governors hired by landowners, reactionary prefects,
third-rate lawyers with dirty feet and plastered with brilliantine,
  liberal officials as dishonest as their bigoted uncles,
a barracks, a seminary, a vacant beach, a brothel!
  Millions of middle-class men and women like millions of hogs
grazing, shoving their way through immaculate buildings,
  among farm houses that are peeling like old churches.
Precisely because you have existed, you no longer exist,
  precisely because you have been responsible, now you are
    irresponsible.
And only because you are Catholic you can't imagine
  that your evil is the entire evil: the root of all evil.
Sink into this lovely sea of yours, free the world.

To A Ghost[21]

Only because you are dead, I've been able to speak to you man
to man
otherwise your principles would not have allowed it.
No one defends you, now: the dead instituted world
whose son and master you were, abandons you.
Startled corpse of an old man, stammering phantom,
lost, you are beginning to sink through the ages:
you are finally my brother, hate and love unite us,
my living body and your cadaver
are joined together by a bond that turns us both into ghosts.
But for a word of reproof uttered against you,
poor sinner, stripped, degraded by death,
made bare and beseeching like an unfledged bird,
how many words must I still suppress in my heart!
You left behind an empty place, and, in that place,
another, untouchable because alive, begins to rule.
But "death shall not reign!" Only in this absurd country
where, beyond either of us, Byzantium and Trent survive,
death reigns: but I am not dead, and I shall speak.

Uncivil Poems

(*April* 1960)

The Stylistic Reaction

Everyone pledges to be pure:
pure in language ... naturally:
a sign that the soul is foul.
It has always been
this way. To lie one need not be obscure.
Monsters, they deceive themselves that death
is the great equalizer! They don't know that it is death precisely
(the alibi of Catholic servants)
that disintegrates, erodes, deforms, decomposes:
as does language.
Death is not order, you arrogant
monopolists of death,
its silence is a language too complex
for you to base your power on it:
it is precisely around it that life

swirls! And you are fearful
of your blessed death, of the chaos it implies:
your unilingualism is a shield!
Language is obscure
not limpid – and Reason is limpid,
not obscure! Your State, your Church,
with your blessing, insist on the opposite.
Infinite are the dialects, the slangs,
the accents, because infinite are
the forms of life:
we must not silence them, we must make them ours.
But you don't want them
because you don't want their history, you arrogant
monopolists of death: poets
speak like priests, and, everywhere

prophetic Cassandras
cry victory – the time for optimism has passed!
They were right from their hiding
places in the parishes.
Now they come back out into the daylight,
croaking the anguish of privilege,
of the hopes imposed
by the power of infinite capital.
Gadda![22] You who are obscure language
and obscure reason,
rebut their self-serving blandishments,
with your limpid intellect!
Moravia,[23] you who are limpid discourse
and limpid reason, resist their malicious
manipulations in the brooding pride
of your neuroses... I am alone,
you are alone. In this struggle which is supreme
because it subsumes all the others,
no one is listening to us.
They would like to reduce man to essence, they
who are chaos! Ah, may the earth split open
under their feet, let them speak
their Esperanto in hell.
All the same, even those whom I esteem and love,
and with whom I share so much
of my soul, know language's external
value as history, as if
history were a forging of oneness, a supernal
point that levels off all the passions,
almost as if its goal were the validation

of souls! No, the history
that is to be is not the one that has been.
It doesn't allow for judgments, it doesn't allow for rules,
it is unrealized reality.
And the contradictory language, if it is the fruit of contradictory
centuries – if it is the fruit of mysterious
origins – let no one forget, will integrate itself
with what is and is not yet.
And its essence as enigma, infinite
richness, will now breach
its every limit, every conventional form.
To burn the institutions,
great hope of those who now groan,
is a hope that cannot anticipate
the real passion that will emerge, nor the new

sounds of their words.
The Catholics should not boast of the greatness
of the past, extortionists that they are. Let them despair.
But the Communists should not accustom their hearts
to renounce and minimize
with Hope: with the greatness of the revolution.
Reaction is mirrored in language.
And the language of their words is the language
of the masters and of their throngs of servants.
By all means, may it be lively and fervid
in judging, in prosecuting, may it be a harangue,
an essay: but if it's the fruit
of bourgeois man – who, old and ugly
in the heart, marches towards new
conquests, – it can't help but express all

mankind, in the wretchedness of its history.
There is no avoiding it, even he who objects
is a wretched, impious,
stupid, cold, satiric man
who subverts even his most earnest
passion, and doesn't believe in anyone else's passion...
And in this, the days of relaxation unite
foe and friend alike: the vile war
of slander, of malice, of the blindness
of the political cell
or the sacristy starts anew: the style
of days gone by returns to the hearts
and to the verses: and it is better to die.
. . . .

To The Sun

No, not by us: you are missed
by those who also live at the level
of the sun, in fullness,
and who, among shacks and mounds of earth,
fields covered with cane-brake and trash,
in this swirling breeze, feel
your absence with different heart.
On shoulders bent by humiliation
they've put back on their coats and scarves,
faded by age, tattered, drenched,
and, leaning against a wall,
tapping their feet on broken pavement,
they wait for the old bus to their tenement,
like mute, impotent inmates.

I am here, in their
world (but always at my unpoetic
level of a man of culture, as if atop
a crumbling wall):
with true heart I feel you are missed, sun.
Above, the desperate sky, the dirty drizzle,
automatons of your arcane strike,
they turn us all into automatons of the hour
and of the century; shoddy eternal forms.
A life of worms,
(where not a people, but all mankind
squirms about wet
– and, seen from your height, seem infinitesimal,
seen through your absence, almost divested
of that life) teems all around me.

I would cry out, stricken as I am
by some strange pain. An obscure
pain, like the one of long ago.
Therefore mythical and impure.
Only the sadness of a hostile day
draws me close to this vast dead life:
this anguish, and my own anguish,
are a fact of life, they resemble each other.
There is no boundary between one form of pain and another.
Sun, in your darkness
injustice once again takes place:
against those who have no
clothes or house, against me; I suffer from the mystical
degradation of my soul. A casual coincidence,
a confusing unawareness with awareness.

At this point, I don't know what
the problem is. I don't know if it matters having any,
on this earth left to
its senseless, perpetual
alternation of sun and cloud.
I don't know whether I can recover my former
anguish, and by what new road,
whether to whet again my reason on hatred,
that the peace in the world at present seems to elude
– whether to remain in the ruins
of the post-war period – or to learn the ways
of contemplation,
in the shadow of a new struggle and the sordid
lure of neo-capitalism, already dominant
once more, and ready to forgive...

I have learned, and how I learned!
as a youth, what I was supposed to be
and what I was supposed to do: everything. Back then
the world of my obsession
was the world of capitalism: I was lost
in it like the flavor in fruit,
like the warmth in your light, sun.
Obedient, sincere, terrified,
I was supposed to be not merely good, but a saint,
not a man, but a giant,
not elegant, but pure, exquisite.
I was supposed to find a language,
to express that intimate, infinite light
that was to be extreme: a naive appanage
of bourgeois leisure, of anti-bourgeois courage.

I have learned, and how I have learned!,
at twenty, to discern the most ardent sentiment
amid the luminous chaos
of all sentiments:
freedom. It had kept silent,
for years, and now it was a painful, spontaneous,
and absolute song. And how
the meaning of our existence has changed!
Of those years, I remember only your light,
high above the solitary
clearings of Friuli[6], above a people without
hope: you glowed pure,
always, you were the harsh light of the Resistance.
At a time when the world was never darker,
you were the harsh light of the future.

I have learned, and how I have learned!,
that after every commitment there is once more
the void, and there needs to be a new commitment:
that every condition gives rise
to another condition, and what we have come to know
through pain and disdain
becomes unknown again, in pain and disdain.
While everyone else with blackmail faith
was filled with the light of their own choice,
I continued along the uncertain road
of knowledge, in the chiaroscuro of history.
Intransigence and pain
were the only guarantees of victory,
and precisely in your sunlight
turned to symbol did I harbor your fury.

And I no longer know now what
the problem is. Anguish is no longer
a sign of victory: the world is in flight
towards its new youths,
we've come to the end of all our road, so have I.
Like every old man, I deny it: it's the sole
consolation for one who, if he hesitates, dies.
By denying the world, I deny its new eras,
or feel towards them indiscriminate fury,
on seeing each one of them
contaminated by a common misery.
You shine above a dream,
blackened sun: one who wishes not to know,
wants to dream ....
....

Fragment To Death

I come to you and I return to you,
sentiment born with the light, with the warmth,
baptized when the wailing was joyful,
identified as Pier Paolo
at the onset of a frenzied epic:
I have walked in the light of history,
but my being has always been heroic,
under your dominion, intimate thought.
In the light of your path
in the dreaded misgivings
of your flame, every true act
of the world, of that history,
coagulated: and there it validated itself,
lost its life to regain it:
and life was real only if beautiful...

The fury of confession,
at first, the fury of clarity later:
hypocrite, it issued forth from you, the obscure
sentiment! And now,
let them condemn my passions,
let them smear my name, let them say I am ill-formed, impure,
obsessed, an oath breaker, dilettante:
you isolate me, bestowing on me the certainty of life:
I am on the pyre, I play my fiery card,
and win, this meager,
immense wealth, I win this infinite,
wretched mercy
that brings me righteous, brotherly anger:
I can do it, because I have too long tolerated you!

I return to you, as an immigrant returns
to his country and rediscovers it:

I made my fortune (in the intellect)
and I am happy, just
as I once was, outside the norm.
A black rage of poetry within me.
A young man's senility.
Once your joy was mixed
with terror, it's true, and now
almost with another joy; a
livid, arid one: my misguided passion.
You truly frighten me now
because you are truly close, within
my state of rage, of dark
hunger, almost the anxiety of a new-born.

I am healthy, as you want me,
neurosis sprouts all around me,
exhaustion desiccates me, but
does not conquer me: at my side
the youth's last light smiles.
I've had all I wanted, by now:
and even surpassed
certain expectations of the world: emptied now,
there you are, inside me, filling
my time and all time.
I have been rational and I have been
irrational: to the end.
And now... ah, the desert hushed
by the wind, the stupendous and squalid
African sun that illuminates the world.

Africa! My only
alternative ....
....

Rage

I go to the threshold of the garden door, a tiny
sunken stone passage on the ground
level, next to the urban
garden that has been there since the days of Mameli,[24]
with its pines, its roses, its chicory.
All around, from behind this paradise of rural
tranquillity, peer
the yellow facades of Fascist
skyscrapers, of more recent buildings:
and below them, across thick panes of glass,
stretches a sepulchral depot. In the bright somewhat
chilly sun, the vast garden slumbers;
at its centre, the white nineteenth-century
country-house where Mameli died,
and a blackbird sings as it schemes and plots.

This humble garden of mine, all
of stone... But I bought an oleander
– my mother's latest pride and joy –
and pots of flowers of every kind,
even a wooden sculpture of a monk, as well
as a docile, rosy and a bit irascible cupid,
purchased at Porta Portese,[25] where we were
looking for furniture for the new house. The colors
are few, the season is so biting: delicate rays
of gold, and greens, all the greens...
Only a dab of red, dark and splendid,
half-hidden, brooding, joyless:
a rose. It hangs humbly
on the adolescent stem, as from a wound,
timid residue of a paradise in ruins...

Close up, it is even more pathetic, it seems like
a poor defenseless and naked creature,
a sheer natural
manifestation found in the air, in the sun,
alive, but of a life that betrays
and humiliates it, almost shaming it
for being so crude
in the extreme delicacy of its floral form.
I move even closer, I smell its odor...
Ah, to yell is not enough, and it is not enough to be silent:
nothing can express a whole existence!
I perform no act... I know only
that in this rose I pause to inhale,
in a single wretched moment,
the odor of my life: the odor of my mother...

Why don't I react, why don't I tremble
with joy, or am I enjoying some sort of pure anguish?
Why can't I recognize
this old link with my own existence?
I know: because in me the demon of rage has already
withdrawn. A trivial, unvoiced, vague
sentiment that intoxicates me:
exhaustion, they say, a feverish nervous
excitation: but my conscience no longer is free.
The anguish that little by little alienates me from myself,
if I let go for a moment,
breaks away from me, swirls with a life of its own,
makes my temples throb wildly,
fills my heart with pus.
I'm no longer in control of my own time...

Once nothing could defeat me.
I was enclosed within my life as in the maternal
womb, in the ardent
odor of this humble, dampened rose.
But I was struggling to come out, there in the rural
countryside, a poet in his twenties, destined to suffer
always, always and desperately, and
desperately to rejoice... The struggle has ended
in victory. My private existence
is no longer enclosed within the petals of a rose,
– a house, a mother, a stressful passion.
It is public. But even the world that was unknown to me
has come nearer, has become familiar,
it has revealed itself, and slowly
it has imposed itself on me, necessary and brutal.

Now I can't pretend not to know this:
or not to know how it wants me.
What sort of love
this relationship entails, what loathsome compromises.
No flame burns in this inferno
of aridity, and this arid fury
that prevents my heart
from responding to a perfume, is a passion's
debris... At almost forty years of age,
I find myself with the rage of a youth
who knows of himself only that he's new,
and rants and raves against the old world.
And, as a youth with no compassion
or decency, I don't conceal
my state of being: I'll never be at peace, ever.

The Wisteria

There it is, was I dead?, on
the bastions of the Warship – as unreal
as this air that I've not known since childhood,
or this language of Italics,[26]
pagans or lackeys of clerics – the shadowy
festoons of the wisterias. The affluent neighborhood
is everywhere decked with them. They arrest the sight,
purple in the purple of clouds and avenues.
An absurd miracle, for a soul
for whom the years truly count,
years that were immortal each time for the soul.
The ones that are now being born are
the dead wisterias, not their barbarian offspring
– I say barbarian if threateningly new
is their being, their warning mute...

Let me reiterate: they are not virginal
to life, they are funereal forms
that duplicate the barbarous ways of speech
without yet possessing
speech, pure purple on green...
I was dead, and meanwhile it was April,
and the wisteria was here, to bloom again.
How delightful is this hue of the cadaver
that covers the retaining walls of the Villa Sciarra,[27]
predestined, foreordained, to the end
of time that becomes increasingly voracious...
Damn my senses,
that are, and have been, so fit,
but never so much so that these recent
ancient blooms do not stir them.

I curse the senses of the living,
for whom, April will return through the centuries: along
with the wisterias, with these lilac pods
quivering in fleshy rows,
almost without color, almost, I'd say, ashen...
And so delicate, against the clay walls
or travertine stone, as mysterious as camomile,
such a friend to hearts that come to life with them.
I curse those hearts that I love so much,
because they don't yet know
life, and neither birth!
Ah, life that is real only has yet
to come: virgin, the wisteria bequeaths
to the unborn alone its charm!

And here am I, with this immaterial
grief in my heart, this involute
self-consciousness that reawakens the moment
the season changes.
A hormonal imbalance which is causing the senses
to go wild? A weakening of the heart
beat, or excessive vital activity
by the brain? Ah, certainly something
that's disintegrating. This flower is a sign,
deep within me, of the kingdom
of transitoriness – of religious
transitoriness – nothing less.
Its joy is a painful joy,
and, in the suffering of that nearly white lilac,
it is the cause of this suffering that's exalted.

But it is ridiculous, I can't
torture myself here over this diaphanous shadow
even though it is fraught with spasms,
this delicate lilac
wave that speckles the ruddy retaining wall
with ingenuous immodesty: an aphasic
feast of natural occurrence!
I cannot: I who for years have preached
that all this does not exist, that it is the act
of an alienated will,
of blindness that knows no remedy other
than to die in the heart
of the world received as a gift at birth,
of an unexamined possession of history,
of a purely rhetorical conscience...

And now, on account of a common wisteria
in bloom at some crossing with Monteverde,[28]
I'm here discussing defeat.
But who is ruining me?
God reborn, the blissful guilt?
Yes, I feel I'm a victim, it's true, but a victim
of what? Of an apocalyptic history,
not of this history. I contradict myself.
I'm trivializing my steadfast passion
for truth and reason.
Passion... Yes, because there is an ancient heart
that pre-exists thought:
and a body – that is either flourishing or wounded,
a poor life never truly sure
of controlling the amorphous life of the nerves.

From this inexplicable friction
emerges the first larva of Passion:
between the body and history, there is this
amazing musical
disharmony, in which what has ended
and what is beginning are the same, and remain
so through the centuries: a fact of life.
The boundary between history and the self
is a twisting divide like a dizzying abyss
beyond which at times, we find the splintered,
erratic, glorious hum
of sensual existence
filled with living entity: in the face of this physical
misery every lived event can only be
deemed irrational...

I don't know what this
non-reason may be, this less-than-reason:
Vico, Croce, or Freud come to my aid
in my aboulia, offering nothing but
myth and science.
Not Marx. His speech changes
only what is already speech, but not the first dawn,
nor the darkness that precedes it, my poor wisteria!
All that lives within you – and within me that trembles for you –
remains a repressed groan
about which we know nothing, about which we can't say.
But is it possible to love
not knowing what that means? Lucky
you, that are pure love, my floral twin,
restored to life in a prenatal world!

Overbearing, fierce,
you are reborn, and at once, in a single night, you cover
an entire wall that's just been raised, a princely
wall of ochre
peeling in the new sun that bakes it...
And you are all I need, with your dark fragrance,
you deciduous creeper, to purify me
of history, like a worm, like a monk:
and I don't want this, I refuse it – parched
in my new rage,
trying to make the flaking plaster
of my new edifice hold.
Something has caused the abyss
between the body and history to widen, it has weakened me,
dried me up, reopened my wounds...

You impudent day-old
plant, I moan over this delusion: I know.
Incomprehension and hate are stronger
by far than what a tired
existence can bear:
which moreover, cannot define love – nor death
its twin – its disintegration
is brought on precisely by old senses
made once more keen by my weakness.
And so, at the sight of the purple that smears
the walls in announcing April and the vast epochs,
I want only to die...
My life holds no more rewards:
the vitality of April won't do,
the will to comprehend seems pointless...

A monster with no history,
a fierce barbarian
who carries out his persecutions
in the free press, in subdued confessionals,
who consumes passion, purity, pain,
who accepts death almost with ironic and somewhat
stoical cruelty, who has no religion
other than to impose a lawful one
with his own rules, who has no love
other than a desire to safeguard
everyone's equality, in good times and bad,
who doesn't know pity,
because for each of us winning
in life is a tacit wager that makes us
blind masters of everything we know:

all this I have discovered
at birth, and it was an immediate source of sorrow:
but an almost glorious sorrow, so complete
was my delusion that I thought a heart
could transform any fact,
from within, into a unifying love:
from Christ to Croce, what a comforting journey!
And then, hope in the Revolution.
And now here am I: the wisteria covers once more
the ruddy surfaces
of a neighborhood that is the tomb for all the passions,
affluent and anonymous, warm
in the April sun that decomposes it.
The world eludes me once more, I don't know how
to control it any more, it eludes me, ah, again it is another...

With new fashions, with new idols,
determined to let itself be corrupted,
the mass, not the people, but the mass
now asserts itself in the world,
and transforms it, on every screen, on every video
it finds a drinking-trough, a pure horde that bursts forth
with pure avidity, with an ill-defined
desire to partake of the feast.
And it comes to rest where the New Capital wants it.
It changes the meaning of words:
those who have spoken with hope until now are left
behind, suddenly old.
This humiliated self-torture, this desperate
surrendering doesn't help one to be
young again! Those who don't speak are forgotten.

You who reappear brutish,
not just rejuvenated but reborn,
nature's sweet fury,
you devastate me because I am devastated
by a series of wretched days,
you lean over my reopened abysses,
pristine perfume over my eclipse,
shattered, ancient sensuality, frightened
compassion, death wish...
I have lost my strength;
I no longer know the meaning of rationality;
my life runs aground
– in your religious transitoriness –
it has fallen into despair sensing that there is
only savagery in the world, and my soul rages.

from POETRY IN FORM OF A ROSE

I

Reality

Ballad Of The Mothers

I wonder what sort of mothers you had.
If they were to see you now at work
in a world unknown to them,
caught up in an endless round
of experiences so different from their own,
what baroque and conformist glances would their eyes hold?
If they were there, while you
write your piece,
or as you submit it to editors hardened
to every sort of compromise, would they understand who
  you are?

Cowardly mothers, in whose face the ancient
fear, that like an illness
disfigures features into a paleness
that clouds them over, that distances them from their hearts,
and snares them in the old moral rejection.
Cowardly mothers, poor wretches, anxious
that the children be acquainted with cowardly ways
to solicit a job, to be practical,
not to offend the privileged,
to protect themselves against any form of pity.

Mediocre mothers, who have learned,
with the bashfulness of young girls, about us
a single, naked significance,
with souls that condemn the world
to give neither pain nor joy.
Mediocre mothers, who have never had
for you a word of love
that was not the sordidly inarticulate love
of beasts, and in it they raised you,
impotent to the true calling of the heart.

Servile mothers, for centuries accustomed
to bowing their heads without love,
to transmit to their foetus
the ancient shameful secret
of contenting oneself with leftovers from the feast.
Servile mothers, who have taught you
how the slave can be happy
by hating those who, like oneself, is in chains,
how, by betraying, he can find bliss
and by doing without saying, security.

Ferocious mothers, bent on protecting
the little that, being bourgeois, they possess,
normality and a wage,
almost, with the anger of one seeking revenge
or is contained by an absurd state of siege.
Ferocious mothers, who have said to you:
Be Survivors! Think of yourselves!
Don't ever have pity or respect
for anyone, nurture in your breast
your integrity of vultures!

There they are, cowardly, mediocre, servile,
ferocious, your wretched mothers!
They are not ashamed to know that you
– in your hatred – are even proud,
if this is not but a valley of tears.
That is how this world belongs to you:
despite contrasting passions, despite being in enemy camps,
you have become as brothers by your profound
refusal to be different: to attest to
the savage pain of being men.

Worldly Poems
(1962)

A Solitary Relic...

June 10, 1962

...

I am a force from the past.
Only in tradition is my love.
I come from the ruins, from the churches,
from the altar-pieces, from the villages
lost among the Apennines or the Pre-Alps
where our brothers lived.
I wander through Tuscolana like a madman,
along the Appian Way[29] like a stray dog.
Or I watch the sunsets, the mornings
over Rome, over the Ciociaria, over the world,
like the first events of Post-History,
which I witness, by virtue of the privilege of a registry official,
from the extreme edge of some buried
age. Monstrous is he who is born
of a dead woman's entrails.
And I, an adult fetus, move about
more modern than all the moderns
in search of brothers that are no more.

II

Poetry In Form Of A Rose

Poem In Form Of A Rose

I've got it all wrong.
Blundering, he balked at the microphone,
with the disdainful uncertainty of the ugly man,

of the gentle poet, that namesake of mine
who still bears my name.
His name was Egoism, Passion.

He got it all wrong, with his stuttering bravura,
answering questions from friends or Fascists,
skinny Colossus of the world of letters.

Interlocutors from Teramo or Salerno,
from Conselice, or Frosinone or Genoa,
and, he, so utterly right,

got everything all wrong.

Back from Paris
– a Spring similar throughout Europe,
menstruation of mud and fevered sun,

or that on the fields (rusty with hues
of veiled plum, and oval greens, with the shade
of the Romance forest, in the background...

Watteau, Renoir – saltpetre
below the strata of garish green, uncivilized)
the sun of that Spring
spread overwhelming pain,

or in these fields: at the feet
of altar-pieces, Apennine reds and the shacks
of the Latin proletariat –

... I've got everything all wrong.
Ah, sign systems
derived amidst laughter, with Leonetti and Calvino,[30]

during the usual stop-over, in the North.
Signs for deaf-mutes, ideograms that shall be
once and for all, international.

The poor Dinka[31] in the depths of the Sudan,
with all the other wretched savages
(one hundred and twenty dialects), may he hold his spear

squarely on his shoulder, like a ski,
tall, sublime naked worm,
grandfather or grandchild,

amidst that drawing that's never been drawn
(except by fanatical Rousseauian
rationalists in Europe

of sycamores and mahoganies
(which I love as much as the most beautiful Christian
monuments: perhaps it's the sun, the calm,

the horror of Africa all around)
bloated and asymmetrical, on green,
a green that's not French, a green
that's not Latin,

– on the new green of the world,
embodied in the forest for millennia.
Don't worry, Dinka,
and you of the hundred and twenty other tribes

speaking the sounds of different lineages,

because here with Leonetti and Calvino
we'll sort out the sign systems
and kiss the dialects goodbye.

I've got it all wrong. Fiumicino,[32]
reappearing from behind clouds of mud,
is even older than I am.

The remains of old Pasolini
over the outlines of the Roman plain... shacks
and heaps of skyscrapers...

He is a fleshy rose of pain
with five flesh-colored roses,
rose cancers in the rose

first: in the beginning was the Pain.
And here it is, One and Five.
The first posterior rose signifies

(Ah, a shot of morphine! help!):

You've got it all wrong, you ugly, gentle man!
The very idea of having blundered! Me!
You understand? Me! The let-down, the come-down...

It's all over: blaspheme, commit suicide,
the river sun of Fiumicino
tells me that I'm full of blinding

sand, of crumbling mire.
Inside the taxi the cancer's petals,
towards resurfaced

Rome, with old Pasolini, knocked-out
by himself; degraded, having lost heart.
And, behind the error in the linguistic question,

flesh-colored petal on petal,
in the Quinary Rose, Pain number Two:
here is the "blunder of a whole lifetime."

You just have to put off a petal and you see it.
Red where it should have been white,
or white where it should have been yellow, as you

wish: and this for a whole lifetime,
which, by some bad luck, allows ONE
SOLE WAY, ONLY ONE FORM.

Like a river whose destiny
to be no other river is contained
in the marvelous, astonishing fact of its
being that river.

It's said that in life many opportunities are missed:
but... Life offers one opportunity ONLY.
I've missed mine entirely.

How can the effects of all this
not be felt in sex, castrating
the son to the last teardrop?

And thus we have the Third Crown of the Cancer.
An invasion of barbarians speaking different languages
(the taxi grazes along embankments, the sharp blades

of sombre grass, from the heart of nights
– mysterious, palustrine, primordial –
abandoned to this lethal sun)

a medieval invasion of Goths or Celts.
This sun that causes migraines in modern
adolescents, university students, middle-class

women, with lipstick and driver's licenses...
poisons the barbarian too... Ah,
he shall rest in the chill of tiny flowering

meadows, absorbed, perhaps, in some
manual labour, never unworthy
of man. Above him, no bell shall toll

beyond the divisions of fallow fields
– pagan, with Priapus, Christian
with the cross – in the Latin town,

the bell that throughout the millennia never rang
at three o'clock in the afternoon.
The reawakening of sex comes before
the Spring: perhaps it's the chill or the sweat

that reawakens the flesh still in its woolen winter
clothes, flesh like that of a dog or horse,
which in its woolliness seems to have the same scorching

softness, flush as fruit and mud-like dryness,
perhaps it's the cold that snakes through
the too-green grass on banks,

or the warmth of the first white sun,
in which the town bell is silent,
and the animals graze as if dreaming...

And the woman, whose nobility
is apparent in the hypocrisy
of her pretence at being simply compliant,

– calling her weakness obedience –
she too is lost in a woman's manual
task, she, among the females...

And she doesn't sing: for never through the millennia
did woman ever sing at three o'clock in the afternoon.

Menstruation in the sun has no odor.
The animals graze as if dreaming...

That Third Pain consists
not in withstanding the terrible desire,
but in deriving from it only obsession.

And, thence, the Fourth Pain,
dominated by death impulses
that rising up from my bowels, it makes me want to bash
my voiceless head against the windows

of the taxi that cruises down
the horrible highway where it is clear
that I am without love, while the barbarous
or miserably bourgeois world is full,
full of love... From century to century

the sun gives migraines and erections – dominating
his nighttime desire, the father urinates
in the little ditch of an ancient division

of fields, the work of pre-Italic and Italic peoples,
in this same circle of the Apennines,
and in woolen sweater

and the first sweat in the chill,
fists on my belly, I ascertain from this sun
the absence of love, down to the last teardrop.

The Fifth Pain is the least expressible
(now that in the Paris press
they misspell my name,

and that with Calvino and Leonetti, Professors
of Modernity in the Universities of the North,
an anthropological era is in sight

which desecrates the dialects!)
now it is quite ridiculous,
without the tears,

in the understanding of its cause:
the delusion of history!
It makes us arrive at death
without having lived,

and, for this, we remain alive
to contemplate it, like a wreckage,
a stupendous possession that doesn't belong to us.

The ridiculous pain of a prisoner,
of a cripple, who sees everything granted to others
in a triumph of endless happiness,

simple as the sunlight with which it mingles.

The Fifth Pain is the awareness
that one sweet morning billions
of living beings shall awake,
as they do every morning of their lives,

to the simple sun of the Europe of the future,
its mulberry trees, its primroses,
– or to the deep sun of India
in the sublime stench of cholera that wafts

over small bodies as naked as spirits,
– or in the shameless African sun
increasingly modern
over the green of death that will frame
the impetuous gift of life,

– or in this river sun of Fiumicino,
that makes of the odor of the mud a feast
of shabby Latin immortality...

Billions of living beings
will awake one sweet morning
to the simple triumph of the thousand mornings of life,

with scorched sweater... with the dampness
of the first sweat... Happy – they –
happy! They alone happy!

They alone possessors of the sun!
The same sun of the barbarian
who invaded in medieval times,

and, from the mountain gorges, from the shadows
of the snows, pitched camp
on the thick, black,
evil and vibrant grass of April banks.

Only he who is not born, lives!
He lives because he will live, and all will be his,
is his, was his!

Rome, spreads out like a
dawn, behind the winding Tiber,
swollen with trees as radiant as flowers,

white gleaming city that awaits the unborn,
her shape as unpredictable as a fire
in the fire of a New Prehistory.

III

Pietro III

The Lack Of Demand For Poetry

Like a sick slave, or a beast,
I wandered through a world assigned to me by fate,
with the slow movement of monsters
that live in mud or dust or in the forest,
crawling on the belly or on flippers ill-suited
for dry land or on membranous wings...
There were embankments all around, and rock beds,
or maybe deserted railway stations in the core of cities
of the dead – with roads and underpasses
of dark night, where all that can be heard
are frightfully distant trains,
and the gurgle of drains circumscribing frost,
in the shadow that has no tomorrow.
And so, as I propelled myself forward like a flaccid worm,
repugnant in its ingenuousness,
something slipped into my soul – as
if on a clear day the sun were to darken;
on the sorrow of the breathless beast
settled yet another, meaner, darker sorrow,
and the world of dreams shattered.
"No one has any demand for your poetry!"
And: "Your time as poet has passed..."
"The fifties have ended for all time in the world!"
"You are fading together with your *Ashes of Gramsci*,[33]
and everything that has been life to you hurts you
like an old wound that reopens and brings death!"

IV

A Desperate Vitality

A Desperate Vitality

I

(Draft, an account, in current "Jargon,"
of what's gone before: Fiumicino, the old
castle, and a first true idea of death.)

As in a film by Godard: alone
in a car that speeds along the highways
of Latin Neo-capitalism – on my way back from the airport –
(where Moravia remained, pure among his traveling-bags)
  alone, "at the wheel of his Alfa Romeo"
    in a sun indescribable in non-elegiac
    verses, because it's celestial
    – the most beautiful sun of the year –
as in a film by Godard:
    under that singular, immobile, bleeding
    sun,
  the canal of the port of Fiumicino
  – a motorboat returning unnoticed
  – Neapolitan sailors in woolen rags
  – a road accident, with a few people gathered around...

– as in a film by Godard: the rediscovery
of Romanticism at the heart
of Neo-capitalist cynicism, and cruelty –
at the wheel
on the road to Fiumicino,

and there the castle (what a sweet
mystery, for the French screenwriter,
in the endless, troubled and secular sun,

this papal monstrosity with its crenels,
above the vine rows and the hedges of the ugly countryside
of peasant servants)...

– I am like a cat burned alive,
crushed under the tires of a tractor-trailer,
hung from a fig tree by young boys,

but still with at least eight
of its nine lives intact;
like a snake turned to bloody pulp,
a half-eaten eel

– sunken cheeks under dejected eyes,
hair thinning horribly on the skull,
bony arms like those of a child
– a cat that won't croak, Belmondo[34]
who "at the wheel of his Alfa Romeo"
in the logic of narcissistic montage,
detaches himself from time, and there inserts
Himself:
in images that have no relation
to the boredom of successive hours...
to the radiance of the slowly dying afternoon...

Death is not
in the inability to communicate,
but in being no longer understood.

And this papal monstrosity, not altogether without
grace – the reminder
of the privileges of landowners,
in reality as innocent as the resignation
of servants –
in the sun that has been,
through the centuries,
for thousands of afternoons,
here, the only guest,

this papal monstrosity with crenellated battlements,
nestled in a marsh of poplar-groves,
fields of watermelons, embankments,

this papal monstrosity, armored
with buttresses the delicate orange color
of Rome, peeling
like Etruscan or Roman edifices,

is about to be no longer understood.

II

(Without fading out, I cut sharply to a scene of me performing an act – never done before – of "cultural industry".)

I, voluntarily martyred ... and
she in front of me on the sofa:
shot, reverse shot, in quick succession,
"You – I know what she's thinking, as she looks at me,
in an exemplary domestic-Italic frequency modulation,
always *a la Godard* – "You are a kind of Tennessee Williams!"
the cobra in the stylish pullover
    (as the stand-in cobra
    skims magnesium in silence).
Then, with more force: "Tell me what you're writing?"

"Verses, verses! I'm writing! verses!
(damned idiot,
verses that she can't understand since she doesn't
know anything about prosody! Verses!)
VERSES NO LONGER IN TERCETS!

        Do you understand?
This is what matters: no longer in tercets!
I have gone back, pure and simple, to the magma!
Neo-capitalism has won, I'm left
on the sidewalk
    as a poet, ah [sob]
    and as a citizen [another sob]."
And the cobra with the ballpoint:
"The title of your work?" "I don't know...
[He now speaks in a low voice, as though intimidated, assuming
the role that the interview, once established, imposes
on him: how it wouldn't take much
for his grim expression
to fade

on the face of a nitwit, condemned to death]
– perhaps...'The Persecution'
or... 'A new prehistory' (or Prehistory)
or...
[And here he rears up, regains
the dignity of civil hatred]
'Monologue on the Jews'...
[The dialogue
falters, like the weak rhythm of a jumbled
octosyllabic verse: magmatic!]
"What does it deal with?"
"Well, it deals with my... with His, death.
It isn't in the inability to communicate [death]
but in not being understood...

(If the cobra only knew
that this is a half-baked idea
concocted on the way back from Fiumicino!)
They're almost all lyrics, whose temporal and
spacial components
strangely consist of a car ride...
meditations at speeds of sixty to one hundred and
twenty km/hour...
with quick panoramic panning, and dolly shots
tracking forwards and backwards,
of significant monuments, or tiny groups
of people, pressing their way
towards an object of their love... of a citizen
(or a user of the road)..."

"Ah, ah – [it's the cobra with the ballpoint who's laughing] –
and...
exactly who is it that *doesn't understand*?"
"Those who are no longer among us."

III

Those who are no longer among us!
Swept away by a new gust of history,
towards other lives, with their youthful innocence.

I remember, it was... for a love
that invaded my brown eyes and my honest trousers,
the house and the countryside, the morning sun and the evening

sun... during the good Saturdays
in Friuli, and the...Sundays...Oh, I can't
even utter this word of the virginal

passions, of my death (played out in a dry
ditch swarming with primroses,
among vines deadened by golden rays, sheltered by dark

farmhouses against a sublime blue sky).

I remember that in that monstrous love
I came close to screaming from pain
for the Sundays when "the sun shall shine

on the sons of the sons!"

I was crying, in my narrow bed in Casarsa,
in the room that smelled of urine and laundry
on those Sundays that shone to death...

Incredible tears! Not just
for what I was losing, in the heartrending
immobility of that moment's splendor,

but for what I would lose! When
new youths – whom I couldn't even imagine,
so much like those who now wear

heavy white woolen socks and English jackets
with boutonnieres – or made of dark
cloth suitable for weddings, handled with filial care,

– would populate the Casarsa of future lives,
unchanged, with its stones, and its sunlight
covering the town in golden water...

In an epileptic fit of homicidal
anguish, I protested,
like someone given a life sentence, by locking myself
in my room,
without anyone's knowledge,
to scream, with my mouth
covered with blankets darkened by burns
of the pressing iron,
the precious family blankets,
on which I nurtured the flowers of my youth.

And one afternoon, or evening, screaming
I ran,
through the Sunday streets, after the game
to the old cemetery, behind the train tracks,
and there performed, and repeated till I bled,
the sweetest act of life,
I, alone, on a little mound of earth,
the graves of two or three Italian
or German soldiers
with no names on the wooden crosses
– interred there since the other war.

And later that night, among the dried tears, the bleeding
bodies of those poor unknowns,
dressed in olive-green garb

appeared in a cluster above my bed
where I was sleeping naked and exhausted,
to smear me with blood, till the sun rose.

I wasn't even twenty – eighteen,
nineteen ... and already a century had passed
since my birth, an entire life

consumed by pain of the idea
that I would never be able to give my love
to anyone except my hand, or the grass in the ditches,

or even the dirt of a neglected grave...
Twenty years, and with its human history, and its cycle
of poetry, a life had passed.

IV

(Resumption of the interview, and confused explanation of the function of Marxism, etc.)

(Ah, mine is just a visit to the world!)

But, let's get back to reality.

[She's here, her worry is visible on her face, but she's softened by proper upbringing, waiting, in the "gray" framing shot, in keeping with the proper rules of French classicism.
A Léger.]

"According to you then" – she says reticently,
nibbling on her ballpoint – "what is the function
of the Marxist?" And she gets ready to take notes.

"With... the tact of a bacteriologist... I'd say [I stutter
as though in a deathly fit]
to move masses the size of Napoleonic, Stalinist armies...
with billions of supporters...
so that...
the mass that calls itself conservative
[of the Past] loses it:
the revolutionary mass, restores it
by rebuilding it in the very act of conquering it...
It is due to the Instinct of Self-Preservation
that I'm a communist!
A movement
on which hinges life and death: to the end of time.

It is to be accomplished very slowly, as when
the leader of a bomb-squad unscrews
the safety catch of a live bomb, and,
for an instant, he either stays in the world
(with its sunlit, modern buildings all around him)
or is forever erased from it:

an inconceivable disproportion
between the two horns!
A movement
that must be carried out with tact, by craning,
stooping, crawling on our bellies,
biting our lips or squinting his eyes
like a bocce player
who, wriggling, tries to control
the trajectory of his toss, to change its course
so it heads towards a solution
that will determine life through the centuries."

V

Life through the centuries...
This then is what
it was – last night...
caught in the brief moment of his moan –
that distant train...

That train that was groaning,
disconsolate, as though surprised to be existing,
(and at the same time resigned – because every act
of life is a point already marked on a line
that is life itself, clear only in dreams)

that train was groaning, and the act of groaning
– incredibly distant, beyond the Apennines
and the Centocelles[35] of the world –
was joined to another act: a chance union,
monstrous, wild,
and so private
that only behind the line of my eyes
perhaps closed, is it possible to envision it...

Mine is an act of love. A love lost in the wretchedness
of a body granted by some miracle,
in the task of hiding, in panting
along a gloomy railway track, in tramping through the mud
of a countryside farmed by giants...

Life through the centuries...
like a shooting star
beyond the sky over gigantic ruins,
beyond the estates of the Caetanis or the Torlonias,[36]
beyond those of the Tuscolanes and the Capannelles of this
world –
that mechanical groaning was saying:
life through the centuries...

And my senses were there listening to it.

I was caressing a disheveled and dusty head,
the blond that we need in life,
in the shape that destiny decrees,
and the body of a colt, agile and tender,
with the rough garments that know a mother's care:
I was performing an act of love,
but my senses were listening:

life through the centuries...

Then the blond head of destiny disappeared
through an opening,
through the opening came the white sky of night,
until against that strip of sky appeared
another head of hair, another nape;
black or perhaps brown, and
in the grotto lost in the heart of the Caetani
or the Torlonia estates
among ruins built by seventeenth-century giants
during endless carnival days,
I was listening with my senses...

life through the centuries...

Many times through the opening set against the whiteness
of the night that stretched
beyond the Casilines of the world,
the head of destiny disappeared and reappeared,
with the mildness of a southern mother
of an alcoholic father, always the same
little head, disheveled and dusty, or already
combed in keeping with the vanity of a working-class youth:
And I,
with my senses listening

to the voice of another love
– life through the centuries –
a pure life rising toward the sky.

VI

(A Fascist victory)

She looks at me pityingly.
"And... well then, you... [a desirous worldly smile,
conscious of her avidity, and the gleaming eyes
and teeth, captivating the ostentation
of slight, uncertain, infantile disdain
towards herself) well then, you must be very unhappy!"

"Eh, (I must admit it)
I'm in a state of confusion, Miss.

On re-reading my typewritten book
of poems (the one we're talking about)
I had the vision... Oh, I wish it were
only a chaos of contradictions – the reassuring kind
of contradictions... No, it's the vision
of a confused soul...

Every fake feeling
produces the absolute certainty of experiencing it.
That was my fake feeling...
the sense of being healthy. Strange! saying it to her
– completely lacking in understanding,
with her doll's face with no lips –
with a clinical lucidity I can now verify
the fact
that I have never enjoyed lucidity of any sort.

It's true that at times it may be enough,
in order to be healthy (and lucid),
to believe that one is... Nevertheless
(write, keep writing!) my present

confusion is the result
of a Fascist victory.
    [new uncontrollable, familiar
    deathly impulses]

A minor, secondary victory.
Easy, even. I was alone:
with my bones, a timid, frightened
mother, and my will.

The objective was to humiliate one already humiliated.
I must tell you that they succeeded,
and without much effort either. Perhaps,
if they had known it would be so simple
fewer of them might have inconvenienced themselves!

(Ah, I speak, you'll notice, using an impersonal pronoun: They!
with the ironic love of the madman towards his own illness.)

As for the results of this victory, they too
don't amount to much: one fewer authoritative
signature on petitions for peace.
Well, *a parte objecti*, it isn't much.
A parte subjecti... Well, let's leave it at that;
I've described too much already,
and never verbally,
my pains are those of a crushed worm
who raises his little head and squirms,
with repugnant ingenuousness, etc.

A Fascist victory!
Write, keep writing: make sure *they* know that I know:

I have the conscience of a wounded bird
that meekly dying does not forgive."

VII

He does not forgive!

There was a soul, among those that had yet
to descend into life
– so many, all of them alike, poor souls –
one soul, in the light of whose brown eyes,
in the modest forelock combed in accordance with a maternal
notion
of male beauty,
burned the desire to die.

He saw it at once, he
who does not forgive.

He took it, called it near to himself,
and, like an artisan,
up there in the worlds that precede life,
he laid his hands on its head
and uttered the curse.

It was a white, clean soul,
like a little boy at his first communion,
wise in the wisdom of his ten years,
dressed in white, in a cloth chosen
according to his mother's notion of male grace,
in his warm eyes, the desire to die.

Ah, he saw it at once, he
who does not forgive.

He saw the infinite capacity to obey
and the infinite capacity to rebel:
he called it to himself, and performed on it
– as it looked at him, trustful,
as a lamb looks at its rightful executioner –
the reverse consecration, as
the light in its gaze
faded, and a shadow of compassion arose.

"You shall descend into the world,
and shall be innocent and gentle, steady and faithful,
you shall have an infinite capacity to obey
and an infinite capacity to rebel.
You shall be pure.
Therefore I curse you."

I still see its gaze
full of compassion and of the slight horror
we feel for one who inspires it
– the gaze with which we follow
one who goes to his death unawares,
and, because of the law that compels both he who knows and he who doesn't,
we don't say anything to him –
I could still see his gaze,
as I walked away
– from Eternity – towards my cradle.

VIII

(Funereal conclusion: with synoptic table – for use of the maker of the "piece" – of my career as poet, and one prophetic glance at the ocean of future millennia.)

"I came into the world
in the Analogic age.
I operated
in that field, as an apprentice.
Then came the Resistance
and I
fought with the weapon of poetry.
I restored Logic, and became
a civil poet.
Now it's the time
of the Psychagogic.
I am able to write only by prophesying
while in the grip of Music
due to excessive semen or compassion."

*

"If now the Analogic survives
and Logic has gone out of fashion
(and I with it:
no one wants my poetry any more),
there is
the Psychagogic
(to the disgrace of Demagogy
always more
in charge of things).
This is how
I can write Themes and Threnodies
and even Prophecies;
ah yes, as a civil poet, always!"

*

"As for the future, listen:
your Fascist sons
will sail
towards the New Prehistory.
I will wait there
like someone dreaming of his own undoing
on the shores of the sea
where life is always beginning again.
Alone, or almost alone, on the old coastline
among ruins of ancient civilizations,
Ravenna
Ostia, or Bombay – it is all the same –
with peeling Gods, old problems
– such as the class struggle –
that
dissolve...
Like a partisan who
died before May 1945,
I will begin to decompose slowly,
in the agonizing light of that sea,
a forgotten poet and citizen."

IX

(Closing Statement)

"My God, what then do you have
on the credit side of the ledger?..."
"Mine? – [a detestable stammering,
            I didn't take the medication, my voice is shaky
                        like that of a sickly child] –
Mine? A desperate vitality."

ASIDES

from ALI BLUE-EYES

Prophecy

To Jean-Paul Sartre who told me
the story of Ali Blue-Eyes.

There came into the world a son
and one day he went to Calabria:
it was summer, and the new
hovels which resembled
sugarbread hives were
empty. As in fairy-tales the color
of hunger. Empty.
Like pigsties with no pigs, in the middle of gardens with no vegetables,
of fields without earth, alongside dry banks. Tilled by the moon, the
fields. The weeds had grown through mouths of skeletons. The Ionian wind
beat the blackened hay
as in prophetic dreams:
and the famine-colored moon
tilled fields that no summer
had ever loved.
And it was in the time
of the son that such love
might be born, but it was not
to be. The son had eyes
of burnt hay, fearless eyes,
that saw all that was evil: nothing
knew he of agriculture,
of land reform, of trade union
struggles, of National Aid Programs,
but – he had those eyes.

Each dark peasant,
every one had abandoned
his new hovel
like a pigsty with no pigs,
in clearings the color of hunger
at the foot of rotund hills
within view of the prophetic Ionian Sea.
Three millennia passed
not three centuries, not three years, and in the malarial air one felt once
again presentience of Greek colonists. Ah, how much longer, laborer of Milan,
will you struggle just for salary? Don't you see how these people venerate you?
Almost like a Master.
They would bring to you,
from their ancient regions,
fruits, cured meats, their
occult fetishes, and laid them
with solemn ritual
between refrigerator and television set
in your twentieth-century bachelorette,
attracted by your divinity.
You, of the state commission,
of C.G.I.L.,[37] you divine ally
in the safe sun of the North.

In the Land of racial
diversity, the moon cultivates
a field that you have uselessly
provided for them.
In their Land of Beasts
Of Burden, the moon
is mistress of souls that you

pointlessly modernized. Ah, but the son knows: the grace of knowledge is a wind which changes course, in heaven. It now blows perhaps from Africa and you should listen to what by grace the son knows. If he then does not smile,

it is because hope for him
was not light but rationality.
And the light of the sentiment
of Africa, that suddenly sweeps
across the Calabrias, be it a sign
without meaning, relevant
in future times! Hence:
you shall put an end to your struggle
for mere salary and armor
the hand of the Calabrians.

Ali Blue-Eyes
one of many sons of sons,
will plow forth from Algiers
on ships with sails and oars.
There will be with him thousands,
like their fathers, tiny-bodied men
with eyes of wretched dogs
on boats launched in the Kingdoms of Hunger. With them will be the children,
and bread and cheese wrapped in the yellow foil of Easter Monday. With them
will be the grandmothers and the donkeys, aboard the triremes stolen from
the colonial ports.
They will land at Crotone or at Palmi,
by the millions, clad in Asian
rags and American shirts.
At once the Calabrians will say
as though from one brigand to another:
"Here are our ancient brothers,
their children, and the bread and cheese!"
From Crotone or Palmi they will
sail on to Naples, and thence
to Barcelona, Salonika and Marseille,
the City of the Underworld.
Souls and angels, mice and lice,
carrying the seed of Ancient History
they will fly before the prophecy.

They always the humble
they always the weak
they always the timid
they always the tiny
they always guilty
they always subjects
they always invisible
they who never wanted to know, they who had eyes only to implore, they who lived like assassins underground, they who lived like bandits at the bottom of the sea, they who lived like the insane in the middle of the sky,
they who created their
laws outside the law,
they who adapted
to a world under the world,
they who believed
in a God servant of God,
they who sang
at the slaughter of kings,
they who danced
at the bourgeois wars,
they who prayed
at labor rallies...

... abandoning the honesty
of peasant religions,
forgetting the honor
of the underworld,
betraying the candor
of barbarian peoples,
behind their Alis
of the Blue Eyes – they will emerge from the underground to kill – they will surface from the bottom of the sea to attack – they will swoop down from the sky to steal – and before arriving in Paris
to teach the joy of living,
before arriving in London
to teach how to be free,
before arriving in New York,
to teach how to be brothers
– they will destroy Rome
and upon its ruins
they will sow the seed
of Ancient History.
Then with the Pope and all the sacraments
they will hasten like gypsies
to the north-west
with the red banners
of Trotsky in the wind...

from THEOREM

The First Paradise, Odetta...

The first Paradise, Odetta, was that of the Father.
There was an alliance of the senses, within the offspring
– male or female –
owing to the adoration of something singular.
And the world surrounding it
had one feature only: the desert.

In that murky and boundless light,
In the circle of the desert, like a mighty womb,
the child enjoyed Paradise.
Remember: there was only a Father (no mother).
His protectiveness
had a mature yet youthful smile,
and slightly ironical, as is the smile of those who protect
the weak, the tender – boy or little girl.

You have lived in this First Paradise
till today; and, being female,
it shall live on in your memory, you shall always revere it.
You will always be, by nature, a worshipper... But before
I come back to you, to warn you of the dangers
of religion, I want to retrace the story
of your brother, who is of the same sex as God.
He, too, in times when he was *truly* young,
(even younger than when in the maternal womb
or when he suckled the first milk from the breast)
lived in the First Paradise of the Father.

The hatred appeared abruptly, without reason.
The womb that was like a sun covered
by balmy, mighty clouds, the womb of that Man
who is vast and singular like the desert,
became like a trouser's dark crotch;
impoverished, it lost innocence,

in suspicion that the whole was only human.
The day had come
when the pure horizon of the desert dissolves
in a silence and in a color less than perfect,
one begins to see the first palm trees,
the first footprint appears, mute among the dunes.

So the child crossed the border of the First Paradise:
which was left behind, in time; in the *dreamed* time,
of a verdant region lined with rows of translucent
birch trees – or in a large provincial town.
The child fell headlong upon the earth,
lost the name of Lucifer and took
the names of Abel and Cain (this is at least true
for certain rose-colored, Mediterranean lands, and for these verdant
ones, where nuns teach this to a secular Odetta).

These lands were the Second Paradise.

There was a mother (adoptive, let us say) who, in your case
owned rich furs bearing the fragrance of early springs.
Her fragrantly earthly mildness
was that of a young, middle-class girl
who doesn't crave all the sweet things for herself,
but for that young boy of hers strolling by her side,
He, too, ineffably scented with the cool fragrance of primroses!

A river flowed (in your case the Po) in that Paradise:
because the house where the "adoptive" parents live,
after the wedding, is always near a river.
Or if not a river, the sea, or a range of hills.

Fruit grew all by itself, bearing wondrous names:
apples, berries, cherries, grapes; and the flowers, the useless
flowers, were no less remarkable, and their names too
were marvelous, primroses, or sunflowers,
or snowdrops, or lilies of the valley, and for feast-days, even
orchids.
The sun was indeed a friendly creature,
made even gentler by the innocent thought that the mother
communicated to her young son, whom she held tightly by the
hand;
and as it was born in the morning, so it died in the evening,
surrendering its place to the stars that the son, obedient,
no sooner saw, then had to abandon to their own silences.

But the mother was not as innocent as he believed!
And so the same hatred, without reason – which had emerged
all by itself, like a fruit or a flower, in the First Paradise –
erupted also in the Second. Our existence
is but a senseless identifying with the living
towards which something immensely ours pushes us.

Thus we became the sinning mother facing the fruit
whose mystery resurrected the days of the First Father
– so much earlier than those of the verdant Paradise of
Lombardy!

Again the sun of the desert glowed
on that tiny apple, desire for modest existence.
The usual everyday sun remained distant,
segregated as in a precipitous December, while the other
marvelously

blazed: measurement against which to measure centuries and
miseries.
The mother, therefore, *who was none other than her own young son*,
with motherly innocence and filial carelessness bit
into that summer fruit. Impetuously, the second father, the adoptive one
– who, next to the first, was like the feeble
sun of winter compared to the sun of First Summers –
followed her example, exiled man of the earth,
easily tempted and easily corrupted.

But we had identified ourselves with him also:
because, by ourselves, we could not exist;
we could exist only if we became the father, the mother.
We sinned with their very mouths, their very hands.
And the First Father even banished us from the Second Paradise.

Two, therefore, the Paradises we have lost!
Fast by the hand of our parents we took to the roads of the world.
Lucifer distinguished himself from Abel, and followed his own destiny
ending in deepest blackness. Abel died,
slain by himself, bearing the name of Cain.
Finally there was one son left, *one son only.*

After many millennia we had the first seeding,
and another millennium after that event
a King was named ruler over the men who had multiplied.
Ah, how many feasts served on fine china! We had to earn our bread,
and this began to take hold of us, and each of us
was lost in a false idea of ourselves, in the present hell.
Along this path your brother Pietro is about to set off.

But why, in presenting to you this Theory of the Two Paradises,
have I spoken of your brother and not you?
It's simple: because without his story, of the male offspring,
there would be nothing to compare your own story to,
and so it would be impossible to even begin to speak of it.

There has not been a female Lucifer, nor a female Abel, nor a Cain:
you, therefore, should have remained in the First Paradise –
or, at least it is the one you should remember, with the true Father.
And so it is: in essence you are immensely older
than your adoptive father, with whom you are in love,
than your adoptive mother, who has the name of Lucia,
than your brother Pietro, model for all existence.

With each of them, to your detriment, you have identified yourself,
and you don't know that it is you rather who is before their births,
who is the one truly obedient to the First Father.
What should matter most, your identity or your existence?
You don't know how to choose, tender Odetta, because you are blind:
in this way you are chosen, in this way you are lived; and you resist,
hopelessly, lost between a recollection that is too beautiful
and a reality that takes you from the dream to madness.

from TRANS-HUMANIZE AND ORGANIZE

I

Trans-humanize and Organize

Press Release to ANSA[38] (*Resolutions*)

I drank a glass of water at three in the morning
while Arezzo seemed to me absolutely detached.
Once I've decided to surrender my primary obligations
(as poet and citizen)
my poems will be *completely practical*
(though I am well aware that without God the practical is
surreal)
As Euripides says: "Democracy consists
of these simple words:
who has useful advice for his country?"
From now on, my advice will be that of a silly moderate.
After my death, no one will miss me:
ambiguity is relevant 'till the Ambiguous lives.

Press Release to ANSA (*Stylistic choice*)

I cease to be an original poet, whose price is lack
of freedom: a personal stylistics is too exclusive.
I'll adopt the tried and true models, to be freer.
Naturally, for practical reasons.

Press Release to ANSA (*Ninetto*[39])

Anghelos[40] is unrecognizable, Savona doesn't recognize him
just as he doesn't recognize Communist China.
Unrecognized, he smiles, but his is a half-smile.
His lightheartedness is his sole inheritance,
it's something the State can tax.
To exist he must be a bystander: his relations
with others are contractual: being a modern youth,
he doesn't believe in myths: and yet, it's well known,
only what is realistic is mythical, and vice versa.
Naturally, he doesn't believe in fables: his life
is a fable made of nothing.
He quickly loses the sense of others:
he forgets their faces. He moves in the world
in gray-green garb like a dog whose jaws are full of kindness.
He is led by the hand by a destiny whose *objective*
goal is nothing practical; the *involvement of an ally*,
should one come along, is well and good, if not, never mind
      (I am an ally):
the *elimination of the enemy* occurs mythically
with fists, or perhaps, I admit it, even with knives.
Negotiation? He protests a little, then resigns himself.
Aggression is an every day thing.
Retributions (reparations and vendettas) are not considered.
No attention is paid to the *process of deterioration*
      or to the *original offense*.
Even less, to the matter of where the *responsibility* lies.
      To the *sacrifice*, perhaps,
if this, right there and then, produces some sort of satisfaction
(which you can pay for even with death). The *suffered aggression*
and the *disgrace*, are things that only Captain Savona looks after.
The cycle of the story is a thread that goes missing in the grass,
as it was for Marlowe's youth. He smiles heroically,
innocent pariah: untouchable, but also unapproachable.

Trans-humanize and Organize[41]

Just before I put on my hearing aid
at an hour when no honest person would write poems.
At an hour when the conscience is least pure.
It's inconceivable that a man should make
such simple discoveries at such a late hour.
I must have been blinded by an outlook that's not so simple.
I was in the foyer of the Istituto Luce[42]
(untouched by the ardent confidence of the verse-maker).
It is strange to notice at such a late hour with my own eyes
things that, for some time,
have probably been daily occurrences.
The crowd pressed against a table with no microphones.
To take the floor you had to stand on chairs.
I'll say it again: it was an hour when poetry's certainty fails.
Indecision was in the air, exhaustion alone can arouse fervor.
To a film-maker, those reticent gazes were a morning's crucial
    discovery.
Who do we turn to to become members of the PCI?
He's the one to whom I address these sentiments, whoever he
    may be.
It's baffling – I say to him – that the most obvious
should take so long to become evident.
The workers want to keep the PCI exactly as it is.
I finally see their desire with perfect clarity.
And here, though this is merely a letter written at the ritualistic
hour when only dishonest poets write poems,
I want to say that this desire is the desire for institutions.
During this brief strike, the workers closest to me,
and the women workers, perhaps for the first
time in their lives equal to the men,
were the embodiment of that desire.
This is what I witnessed. Some youths, bystanders,
were asked to speak in support of it, which, one by one,
    they did.

A provincial deputy, a Christian Democrat, also spoke.
Advising good manners. For the rest, he learned
to say everything in other words; that is, to say *nothing* at all.
It's true, he also spoke of the possible *difficulties*: a polite way
of saying that not all the demands could be met.
A polite way of saying that good will alone might have to do.
Moreover, because provincial politeness can also provoke
he said that ours did not constitute a political assembly.
And suddenly, some young men with ragged beards,
and bumpy foreheads, like beasts of burden,
began to shout against the provocations, their provocations.
These men were just what they seemed to be, however.
They howled: "Down with democracy, up with the revolution!"
'Till hysteria took hold.
And they would not be restrained. Their extremist cry
is what saved them, like a drug that shuts off reality.
Pale, protuding cheek-bones, hard, bulbous foreheads,
and mustaches twisted at right-angles, the color of tobacco.
With them, though not as young, were mingled intellectuals,
with whom they have in common only a pallor, an indignant voice.
As if some specter had descended on that great hall,
invading some, leaving the rest empty.
The young extremists, and the no longer young, became
transfigured by their own shouts which, like a daily deliverance,
they could not control.
The workers remained patient. Then they lost patience
and almost booted them out. But, then they held back.
Good sense prevailed, defeated earlier, it seemed, by other
good sense.
And so, with my own eyes, I saw the laborer with calloused hands
pounce on the hollering academic, for the first time.
The whole scene was watched by a Communist parliamentarian;
a wily, young character, who remained controlled

as well as any worker, while those other damned fools howled.
And, when another worker, out of sheer frustration,
also began to holler and raise his hands,
he, the Communist, continued to stare pensively at that roughneck
with blood-shot eyes.
I too was silent and contemplative. But for different reasons:
how much do I resemble those howling imbeciles!
Perhaps as much as the Piedmontese parliamentarian resembles
    the workers.
My extremist cries are more articulate, less senseless, perhaps.
Nevertheless, and I'm not writing this as an exercise to soothe
my conscience, or to confess my faults for the *n*th time.
Nor do I believe that I'm drawing the hasty conclusions –
rhetorical simplifications – we find at the core of every institution:
even this one, which the workers want to keep as is.
I write this to say that from now on I'll muffle
my scruples, from now on I'll blame only myself.
Do I or don't I love institutions? Isn't that the crucial point?
So, why fight that other truth
that I am compelled to love, obliged as I am to live on the margin
of institutions, like a bandit?
I'll carry out one more act of cowardice. I'll re-enter the ranks.
If I could renew my membership in the PCI, I'd do it.
    And I'd conduct myself
accordingly, with loyalty, making it easier on my conscience.
It's not news that a man must choose
between two compromising lives, and gives in. As it happens,
I have always opposed the PCI with fervor, waiting
for answers to my objections, in order to proceed dialectically!
No answer arrived: a fraternal remark
was misconstrued as a blasphemous rebuttal.
But was it a mistake on my part to see it as banal injustice?
Institutions are unjust. So be it!

Since only institutions guarantee a rapport between these
workers and me.
I'm not speaking of the PCI alone, but also of all that went before
through millenary history that binds me to them.
The workers' wish is to have trustworthy commandments from
a father: they,
who showed great courage in liberating themselves
from the ancient
father, substituted him, thereby achieving the only freedom
they now have.
Let it be clear: this pure and simple idea of seeking
membership today, at almost forty-seven years of age, in the PCI,
might not materialize only because I may still be unable
to take a vow
of chastity: but also because the controversy continues,
since I know I'm incorrigible in my mania for truth
(though I can't say if it is truth, or merely the love of it:
but certainly
it is a mania: a self-emulation, perhaps, my fondness for being
one of the elite, with freedom to choose between commonness
and idealism).
And so, for the love of contradiction, or as a consolation, I must
consider the opposite hypothesis: that is, this pure and simple
act of a membership, cannot be passed off as mere calculated
hypocrisy on my part.*
It may also be my way of achieving the equilibrium, that binds me
deeply and naturally to these workers, just how I don't know.
I betray a pact of loyalty – the one I've made with myself,
the idealist –
because it seems more just to me to enter into a pact of loyalty
with the workers, and with their Party, exactly as they want it.

* In Italy, instead of a Gaullist victory, we've had a Communist victory.

I read their modest human desire, (oh, there is no doubt about that)
in the darkening air of the waning day through the only window.
I always saw them, lost, each in his cell, in his workshop,
or stock-room; shackled to his fate, patient and poor,
sustainer of families, cheerful provider of that "loaf of bread."
That same peace towards all things, souls or editing-machines,
events of the world or film, which I positively noticed in them
on those working afternoons, on those sacred mornings
    without history,
I saw again today. My sight can only pick up how
    imponderable they are
– bisons or ants, dromedaries or blackbirds,
or all of these at once – those facial features wasted
by the monotonous misery of a life immersed in one experience,
and not free to choose, as it lives out its fate.
Their knowledge does not reflect reality, but a reality.
And it is a deplorable and absolute knowledge, cowardly
    and powerful.
Knowledge that can only spawn institutions, deplorable
    and cowardly
that seeks only absolute power. Becoming a member of the PCI
would mean collaborating in that process, by renouncing the heroic
and privileged knowledge that dares to reflect a greater reality
and to defend us against inexorable fate.
I could still do this, in other places perhaps or in other quarters.
Ah, it's only natural that I should have to adapt to this dissociation.
Every thought suggests it; every reckoning, every degradation:
I'll be two persons: hushed up and official in action, alone
and critical in writing poems. Is this not the double life
I always sought – perhaps with some justification?
It's no accident that the sacred and anointed hand of Saint Paul
on my back nudges me in this direction.
The temporal equivalent of transcendence, is it not organization?

The howling intellectuals will find here something to be
    indignant about
(sustained by the shadow of Zhdanov[43] about whom they know
    nothing)
having drawn my conclusions from the color of the waning day
on these faces inflamed by the world of action,
as it merges with the other face of the sky.
But our world is schizoid, dear friends, dear PCI
functionary, to whom I address this letter.

II

(Filthy) Charta

Lines Of The Testament

Solitude: you've got to be very strong
to love solitude; you need good legs
and uncommon stamina; you can't run the risk
of a cold, influenza or sore throat; you can't be afraid
of robbers or assassins; if walking is required
for the entire afternoon or even all evening
you must be able to do it without flinching; there is no place
to sit; especially in winter; wind blowing over the wet grass,
and with the big stones, damp and muddy, amongst the garbage;
there really are no comforts, there's no doubt,
apart from having a whole day and a night before you
with no obligations or limits of any kind.
Sex is a pretext. Whatever the number of encounters
– and even in winter, in streets abandoned to the wind,
among stretches of garbage piled against distant buildings,
there are many – they are but moments of solitude;
the warmer and livelier the graceful body
that anoints with semen and goes on his way,
the colder, more deathly are the deserted derelict surroundings;
that's what fills you with joy, like a miraculous wind,
not the innocent smile or dark arrogance
of he who then goes on his way, he brings with him a
youthfulness
that is hugely young; and in this he is inhuman,
for he leaves not a trace, or, rather, he leaves just one
which is always the same in all seasons.
A boy in his first loves
is none other than the world's fecundity.
It is the world that in this way arrives with him; appearing
and disappearing, like a changing form. Everything else remains
intact,

and you can walk through half the city, you'll never find him
again;
the act is completed, its repetition is a ritual. Therefore
the solitude is still greater if an entire crowd
waits its turn: in fact the number of disappearances increases –
to go away is to flee – and what comes after looms over the
present
like a duty, a sacrifice to the desire to die.
Growing older, however, you begin to feel weary,
especially at the moment when the supper hour has just passed,
and for you nothing's changed; so you come close to shouting
or weeping, and that would be shocking if it weren't just out of
tiredness,
and perhaps hunger too. Shocking, because it would mean
that your desire for solitude could no longer be satisfied,
and so what will become of you, if that which is not considered
solitude
is the real solitude, the one solitude that you can't face?
There is no supper or lunch or worldly satisfaction,
that's worth an endless walk in the poorest streets,
where you have to be wretched and strong, brothers of the dogs.

APPENDIX

The Ideological Dreams

(*An essay*, 1971)

The Ideological Dreams

At what point did History begin?

Certainly no viable hypothesis can be attempted in this regard, even in these pages dictated by a "Heretical Empiricism" replete with fears but also recklessness.

But why not? I could say that History had its origin the moment man stopped living only and started to live by pretexts. That was inevitable, in distinguishing himself from the animal state, etc. etc.: nevertheless the moment living began to be a conscious act *or to be translated entirely into any kind of interpretation of reality whatever, certainly, at that point, instead of an innocent dream, a horrible dream started; instead of a dream made of visions, a dream of pretences, of excuses that made living possible, or filled up one's life somehow: in this way it began to appear as a void (while it is evidently a whole). The years, the days, the minutes began to require or demand to be "filled", that is, to be lived as the fulfilment of certain rules: on this the human fraternity has nourished itself with great voracity. Underneath it all, in the various moments of the historical dream, life continued naturally to have certain real "qualities". Never, never once have men truly tried to understand them. They kept transforming the "qualities" into pretexts that "make one dream inside the dream": reducing life (irreducible by definition) to a "quality of life". What does this "quality of life" consist of? First and foremost, it comprises a succession of obligations: communities, societies, institutions, rights, are merely the by-products of a kind of game that distracts us from that life which is never removed from death. Even the life of children is, by deduction or immaturity, empty: so they fill it with play. Their play (which, however, is a preview of the other game that awaits them) is joyous and vital: perhaps even the Game of History has been (at some inauspicious time) filled with joyous vitality; but because it was in essence a sacrifice, it couldn't avoid degenerating, thus becoming what it is, History, with its obligations and its blackmail.*

Looking at it dispassionately, our life is but the application of the principles of the "quality of life" typical of our historic period. It is like a paranoid system. There is no incoherence in it. The authentic is always absent, because even if something approaching the authentic (however profound or unexpected) happens, it is no more than the attainment of what our "quality of life", conscious of its own violence, accepts as contradictory or anarchic.

Realization of this gives rise to the ideological dreams of palingenesis, *that is, dreams that reconstitute a genuine quality of life. Imminently, however, these ideological dreams become once more part of the Game of History: as a matter of fact, precisely because they are new or innovative, they force us into the game with even greater aggressiveness and violence. They generally equate aggressiveness and violence with the "right" of a historical society (the one which they oppose): but then what do they do? They immediately hypothesize another society, with other qualities of life that are, nevertheless, mere qualities of life, hence "to be filled".*

Normally ideological dreams are born from what, according to the rules of the game, appears to be and passes itself off as reality: they are real in that they are generated and nurtured by a real necessity. For example, the Marxist dream is an ideological dream of this kind.

At other times "ideological dreams" are entirely, totally unreal; they are (and those who dream know it) founded entirely and totally on pretexts.

While in the "long term" of the Game of History what carries true weight are the "real" ideological dreams ("real" relative to the idea of reality that arises from the historical dream), in the "short term", often those that succeed, even if theirs is only a short-lived success, are the "unreal" ideological dreams, that is, the totally invented dreams, constructed entirely from nothing, perhaps for reasons that are, as they say, futile and abject....

* * *

... What life could be without history *is naturally unthinkable or impossible to talk about: what more could I possibly do, in the morning, if not wake up, get out* of a bed, *read* the newspapers, *have* daily thoughts, *as a whole, do what my quality of life allows or even prescribes, surprising and absolutely unheard of as that might be? I have no alternative. The Game of History allows no alternatives except other games of history. I must absolutely invest the absolute act of living with a* pretext, *that is naturally so prosaic, so inferior, so substandard, so bare, so disappointing, with respect to its task of what "should transpire" in time.*

Death puts an end to all kinds of pastimes which are often ferocious. More than other human activities, literature appears more clearly as a game: in fact, it is a game by definition. At least, it is certainly less serious than the other pragmatic or non-pragmatic activities imposed by history.

But, together with religious experience, literature is the only activity that (this always in historical terms) can let us visualize, or at least consider what life without history might be.

In spite of this, literature is also the least comprehensible human activity outside of history: it entrusts the possibility of being understood entirely to specific "ideological dreams", outside of which it is dead word....

AFTERWORD

Prophecy Versus Memory: Towards a New Pre-history*

[T]ogether with religious experience, literature is the only activity that (this always in historical terms) can let us visualize, or at least consider what life without history might be.

PIER PAOLO PASOLINI
The Ideological Dreams

The selections in this volume are drawn from Pier Paolo Pasolini's mature poetry. They comprise poems from *La religione del mio tempo*, 1961, (*The Religion of My Time*), *Poesia in forma di rosa*, 1964, (*Poetry in Form of a Rose*), *Ali dagli occhi azzurri*, 1965, (*Ali Blue-Eyes*), *Teorema*, 1968, (*Theorem*), *Trasumanar e organizzar*, 1971, (*Trans-humanize and Organize*), a late introduction, *Al lettore nuovo*, 1970, (*To the new reader*), and key passages of a pivotal essay, *I sogni ideologici*, 1971, (*The Ideological Dreams*).† The sequence follows a dense itinerary that focuses on revealing Pasolini's prophetic strategy, its advent, its evolution, and its originality and efficacy, in the context of the mnemic civil world in which we live.‡

---

* *A slightly modified version of this essay was first read at a symposium,* Pasolini: Heretical Imperatives, *held at the University of Toronto, June 9, 1990.*

† *La Religione del mio tempo*, *Poesia in forma di rosa* and *Trasumanar e Organizzar* are poetry collections. *Ali dagli occhi azzurri* is a collection of varied writings by Pasolini. *Teorema* is a novel from which Pasolini drew the story for his film of the same title. *Al lettore nuovo* is Pasolini's introduction to a paperback selection of his poems, *Poesie*, 1970, (*Poems*). All books originally published by *Garzanti Editore*. *I sogni ideologici* appeared in *Nuovi Argomenti*, no. 22, Roma, April/June, 1971, pp. 20–24.

‡ The working title of this selection of works by Pasolini was *Ali Blue-Eyes and Other Prophecies*; the present title, *Pier Paolo Pasolini: Poetry*, was adopted on the advice of Pasolini's heirs.

That we live in mnemic times, in a memory-oriented world, is easily substantiated. Suffice it, in a scant note of this length, to quote Claude Levi-Strauss, who, in a recent interview again stated it in plainest fashion:

> *"Nous utilisons toujours l'Histoire pour comprendre le passé, expliquer le présent, façonner l'avenir."**

But Pasolini stood against this unified image of our age. His poetry is witness to his profound alienation from history. And indeed, at the height of his power, we find Pasolini shackled to his battle, though the conflict had begun for him much earlier.

In *The Ashes of Gramsci*, 1954, Pasolini uncovers that Gramsci, the valiant opponent of Fascism, had been buried in the English Cemetery in Rome. Gramsci, an exile in his own country, even in death, becomes, for Pasolini, the buried evidence of a modern society's brutal intolerance towards conscientious and just dissent:

Here they are,

the wretched enjoying the evening. And potent
in them, the defenceless, through them, the myth
is reborn ... But I with the conscious heart

of one who can live only in history,
will I ever again be able to act with pure passion
when I know our history is over?

(translated by NORMAN MACAFEE)

* We are always employing History to understand the past, explain the present, and to shape the future.

Finding his society vehemently restrictive, elitist, manipulative and punitive, Pasolini is forced to choose against it: *"our history is over"*. This crisis with history, the conviction that history, in fact, holds no salvation, no freedom, for the disinherited, the wretched of the earth, the disadvantaged classes, and anyone who dares discover himself to be different from the norm either in flesh or thought, engenders one of the most radical and pervasive attacks on any society by a 20th-century artist.

In *The Religion of my Time*, which is where our selections begin, Pasolini breaks, from his earlier civil language, into an epigrammatic vein, admonishing his nation, his contemporaries, the church, and even his own father's ghost. The book displays such extreme dexterity that it succeeds in giving an altogether new image to his work. The five *"Uncivil Poems"* that close this collection are despairing in tone:

> *I have lost my strength;*
> *I no longer know the meaning of rationality;*
> *my life runs aground*
> *– in your religious transitoriness –*
> *it has fallen into despair sensing there is*
> *only savagery in the world, and my soul rages.*
>
> (*The Wisteria*, translated by ANTONINO MAZZA)

But despairing as these tones are, something remarkable emerges in them the moment when its disheartened, demoralized protagonist recognizes in a wisteria's archaic blooms a continuity untouched by history. "*Biology*", writes George Steiner, "*our elementary intuitions ensure the existence of a primordial continuity between the prehistoric ancients and ourselves.*"

The unexpected discovery of this continuity of the self in history contiguous with the irrational, archaic life force of a "*floral twin*" that bursts forth, suddenly born, is a vision that has significant consequence in all of Pasolini's future works. Prehistoric life doesn't rely on time, on memory, on the past to realize its vitality or to maintain its integrity. So also it must have been for archaic man, who, in facing the angst of ontological and existential oppression and perdition, had no recourse to the past, nor to history, relying instead on the future itself as his ally; therefore, on presentiments, premonitions, and prophecies.

In *Poetry in Form of a Rose*, haltingly, but with renewed formal and stylistic vigor, Pasolini, against the rational order of the victorious few, posits the concept of a new prehistory. Contrary to the contemporary reliance on the past, he has recourse to the radically archaic practice of prophesying, and everything that this change in the direction of the semantic vector of knowledge entails.

The reader of these poems, however, should not confuse the irrational and the prehistoric in Pasolini with the wave of irrational nihilism that invaded the works of the American Beat poets, with whom he has sometimes been erroneously associated. Pasolini's works are imbued with learned tradition, from Virgil to Dante, from the poetry of Michelangelo to the dissenting voice of Giordano Bruno, to name only the most obvious of his precursors. Furthermore, his embracing the archaic past is not a nostalgia for the past, but a search for a poetics of hope.

This new freedom, that sweeps wide before Pasolini's imaginative horizon, acquired through the introduction of the prophetic dimension, allows Pasolini, henceforth, to project future victories in ever larger canvases. Therefore, in apocalyptic poems, such as the two *Asides*, in part three, where, the first develops a metaphor for third world emancipation, the second radicalizes the myth of Eden in a way that should make of Pasolini an original feminist writer in his own right.

Pasolini's canvases became ever broader as he crossed into

cinematic art, and through his heretical pieces which he continued to publish with regularity in *Corriere della Sera*, Italy's most widely read national daily; and in a reportedly six thousand page novel, *Petrolio* (*Gas*), which was left incomplete at the time of his tragic death. *Trans-humanize and Organize*, however, remains by far the most heretical of Pasolini's poetry collections.

Certainly to decipher Pasolini's entire work in a fashion of unity may be impossible. Still, many view Pasolini's contribution to poetry as his greatest achievement. The essay, *The Ideological Dreams*, stresses his faith in those human dreams that are "pure fiction", not based on historical necessity. And it is interesting to point out how Pasolini's "*dreams of pure fiction*" are very similar to what Northrop Frye has referred to as "*the instinct of hope*," which, "*rooted in the human mind, is closely related to the literary, in that all hope is based on fiction, and though having no facts to go on, it is where the creative impulse takes over.*"

Through Pasolini's prophetic strategy we again know the universe of dreams as temporally much more ancient, and statistically extremely vaster and more various. Like Rilke, Dürer and Picasso, Pasolini seems to have penetrated the intimate penumbra of the pulsating human conscience, an inexorably resilient conscience, whose strides in the latter part of our century are unprecedented.

Dream before language, prophecy before memory, Pasolini's poetic itinerary attests to the inherent resolve of even the most silenced and excluded impulses, to overcome any form of hegemony and oppression over the human spirit. His visionary contribution to 20th-century poetry make Pasolini – a force from the past, more modern than all the moderns – one of the most representative voices of our time.

ANTONINO MAZZA
Toronto, 1990–91

NOTES

1. *This essay is Pasolini's own introduction to a paperback selection of his poems published in 1970.*

2. *PCI:* Pronounced/*pē chē*/; Partito Comunista Italiano (Italian Communist Party).

3. None of the poems from that collection appear in this translation.

4. *Petrarca, Francesco (1304–1374):* Poet, first of the great humanists of the Italian Renaissance.

5. *Carducci, Giosue (1853–1907):* Poet; moved away from Romanticism and towards Classicism; introduced Greek and Latin classical metre to Italian poetry. (Nobel Prize, 1906).

6. *Pascoli, Giovanni (1855–1912):* Poet, author of poems of mythical inspiration. (*Myricae*).

7. *D'Annunzio, Gabriele (1863–1938):* Novelist, playwright and poet, in whose work the cult of beauty merges with a Symbolist style of vast refinement.

8. *Hermeticism:* 20th-century Italian poetry movement, best represented by Ungharetti, Giuseppe, 1888–1970, Quasimodo, Salvatore, 1901–1968, (Nobel Prize, 1958) and Montale, Eugenio, 1896–1981, (Nobel Prize, 1975).

9. *Longhi, Roberto (1890–1970):* Art historian and editor of the cultural magazine *Paragone*.

10. *Leonetti, Francesco (b. 1924):* Is a playwright and poet.

11. *Roversi, Roberto (b. 1923):* Is a poet and critic.

12. *Arcangeli, Francesco (1910–1969):* Was a poet.

13. *Gatto, Alfonso (1909–1976):* Was a poet and journalist.

14. *Casarsa:* Town in *Friuli*, north-eastern region of Italy.

15. *Contini, Gianfranco (b. 1912):* Romance philologist and eminent 20th-century Italian scholar.

16. *Zibaldone:* Title of the diary-notebook kept by the foremost Italian Romantic poet, Giacomo Leopardi (1798–1837).

17. *Osoppo:* Town in Friuli. *Partito d'Azione:* one of the several parties that formed the anti-fascist Resistance.

18. *Gramsci, Antonio (1891–1937):* Founder of the Italian Communist Party (1921). He was arrested in 1926, and remained imprisoned until his death. His prison notebooks and letters on problems of culture, history, politics and philosophy, published after the defeat of Fascism, profoundly affected the political and cultural life of post-war Italy.

19. *Via Cassia:* Ancient Roman road.

20. *Waste land:* Pasolini uses English here, an obvious allusion to T.S. Eliot's well-known poem. (Italics mine).

21. *To a ghost:* The ghost is Carlo Pasolini, the poet's father.

22. *Gadda, Carlo Emilio (1893–1973):* Italian novelist; best known for *Quer pasticciaccio brutto de via Merulana*, an influential novel for its linguistic and stylistic innovations, in which the world is represented as a "pastiche," a chaos, that defies any logical explanations.

23. *Moravia, Alberto (1907–1990):* Leading Italian novelist with whom Pasolini, beginning in 1966, coedited *Nuovi Argomenti*, Italy's most prestigious literary journal. They were close friends, and together they traveled throughout the Far East and Africa.

24. *Mameli, Goffredo (1827–1849):* Author of the Italian national anthem, *Fratelli d'Italia* (1847). Belonged to the generation of soldier-poets of the Italian Risorgimento. He fell very young while defending Rome.

25. *Porta Portese:* The market in Rome.

26. As in the language of the Italian people.

27. *Villa Sciarra:* A park in Rome above Trastevere.

28. *Monteverde:* Affluent avenue in Rome.

29. *Appian Way:* Ancient Roman road. *Ciociaria:* Region to the south-west of Rome.

30. *Leonetti, Francesco (b. 1924):* See note above. *Calvino, Italo (1923–1985):* Italian novelist. Both taught at universities in France and wrote for the literary and political journal *Officina*.

31. *Dinka:* One of the several indigenous groups that inhabit southern Sudan. Also the language of the Dinka people.

32. *Fiumicino:* Coastal suburb of Rome, location of Leonardo da Vinci airport.

33. This collection of verse bolted Pasolini onto the national stage as a major new voice. The identification of civil poet, as the author of *The Ashes*, became a burden to Pasolini in his later writing.

34. *Belmondo, Jean-Paul:* French actor cast in several of Jean-Luc Godard's films.

35. *Centocelles, Tuscolanas, Capannellas and Casilinas:* All refer to the world of the underprivileged classes.

36. *Caetanis and Torlonias:* Refer to the wealthy class, the landowning families.

37. *CGIL:* Confederazione Generale Italiana dei Lavoratori, the Labor Union of the Italian Communist Party. There are three major labor unions in Italy, each associated with a major political party.

38. *ANSA:* Agenzia Nazionale Stampa Associata (National Press Agency).

39. *Ninetto Davoli:* Pasolini's lover; starred in several of his films.

40. *Anghelos:* A contraction of the words *angelo* (Angel) and *angheria*; from the Greek Αγγαρεια, (vexation), a necessary burden dictated from above.

41. *Trasumanar: Trasumanar significar per verba/Non si poria* [Dante] (*The meaning of Trasumanar cannot be expressed in words*). Expresses intense spiritualization, towards transcendence. [From *umano: human*, with prefix *tras-* or *trans-*]. Trans-humanize and organize: to organize beyond the merely practical.

42. *Istituto Luce:* Literally, Light Institute; Italy's national film Institute. Luce: light, in contrast to, acciecato: blinded. Pasolini obviously makes use of its semantic value.

43. *Zhdanov, Andrei Aleksandrovitch (1896–1948):* Member of the Supreme Soviet (1937); Commissar in charge of enforcing Stalin's strictures regarding cultural expression.

A NOTE ABOUT THE AUTHOR

Pier Paolo Pasolini was born in Bologna on March 5, 1922, and graduated from its University. His first poetry collection, written in Friulian dialect, appeared in 1942, following his evacuation during World War II to Casarsa (Friuli), where he participated in the partisan resistance with the peasants, from whose ranks his mother had come, and where in 1945 his brother lost his life. His own life was soon thrown into total disarray when his homosexuality became a public scandal, and, in 1949, in abject poverty, he and his mother sought refuge in Rome.

Pasolini's move to the slums of Rome, necessitated by his slave wages as a part-time teacher, was converted into his first major poetry collection, *The Ashes of Gramsci* (1957), and two novels, *The Ragazzi* (1954), and *A Violent Life* (1959), which led to numerous obscenity charges from both state and church. These charges seem quite absurd today, but at the time they were a source of profound anguish, arousing feelings of persecution in Pasolini.

The Religion of My Time was published at this juncture, at a time of enormous literary activity, when, harassed by the judiciary, he was definitely contemplating his crossing into cinematic art, which he did with *Accattone* (1961). Other books followed, *Poetry in Form of a Rose* (1964), *Ali Blue-Eyes* (1965), *Teorema* (1968), *Trans-humanize and Organize* (1971) and more than forty other volumes of poetry, fiction, and cultural and social criticism.

During fifteen years as filmmaker, Pasolini made over twenty films. His best known are *Mamma Roma* (1962), *The Gospel According to Saint Matthew* (1964), *Hawks and Sparrows* (1966), *Oedipus Rex* (1967), *Teorema* (1968), *Pigsty* (1969), *Medea* (1969), *The Decameron* (1971), *Canterbury Tales* (1972), *Arabian Nights* (1974) and *Salò: The 120 Days of Sodom* (1975).

Pasolini was murdered on a beach in Ostia, near Rome, on November 2, 1975.

A NOTE ABOUT THE TRANSLATOR

Antonino Mazza, poet, translator and editor, was born in Calabria, Italy and came to Canada in 1961. He studied at Carleton University, the Scuola Normale Superiore in Pisa, and the University of Toronto. He has taught at the University of Ottawa, and at Queen's University, Kingston, Ontario. As editor he has been associated with *Anthos* (a magazine he co-founded in 1978), *Vice Versa* and *Gamut International.* He is the author of an acclaimed translation of Eugenio Montale's *Ossi di seppia – The Bones of Cuttlefish* (1983). His most recent publication is an LP of original poems, with music by Aldo Mazza, *The Way I Remember It* (1988). He lives in Toronto.